Living in Mexico

Alvino E. Fantini
Beatriz Céspedes de Fantini

Fourth, Revised Edition

PRO LINGUA ASSOCIATES

Published by Pro Lingua Associates
20 Elm Street
Brattleboro,Vermont 05301 USA
802-257-7779 800-3664775
SAN 216-0579

ISBN 0-86647-105-7

This book was originally developed by The Experiment in International Living, Brattleboro, Vermont, as part of its Orientation Development Project. The initial research and development for this project was supported with funds provided by the U.S. Information Agency under the President's International Youth Exchange Initiative. Pro Lingua is grateful for permission to publish this edition.

We also thank Peter de Jong, former Secretary General, The Experiment in International Living, and Barbara Baer de Gomez, Director, The National Office, the Mexican Experiment in International Living, for reviewing the original edition of this document, as well as The Experiment in International Living offices worldwide for identifying the content areas covered in this country-specific series. The staff of the original development project was: Beatriz C. Fantini, writer; Alvino Fantini, director and editor; Janet Gross, production assistant.

Thanks are also appropriate to Senator Patrick J. Leahy of Vermont, a champion of international education and understanding on the Senate Foreign Operations Subcommittee, for his thoughtful foreword.

This edition was edited by AA Burrows. Designed and set by Judy Ashkenaz of Total Concept Associates in Brattleboro, Vermont, using Palatino text and Mistral display types. Illustrations by Maisie Crowther. Mrs. Crowther's illustrations are supplemented by clip art from Art Explosion 40,000 Images by Nova Development © 1995.Cover design by AA Burrows. Printed and bound by BookCrafters of Chelsea, Michigan.

The photographs used in this book are courtesy of the Mexican Government Tourist Office and are copyrighted by the artists. We appreciate the generosity of the Tourist Office.

Fourth, revised edition 1999
Printed in the United States of America

Foreword

Travelers exploring a new country for the first time will find that a few minutes preparation can make all the difference between a rewarding and enjoyable trip — and disaster.

To the busy traveler, this series of very readable and entertaining guides provides a brief introduction, maps, vital statistics, a little history, and a lot of practical advice that instill a sense of security from the time you arrive at the port of entry.

In the brief time it has taken you to familiarize yourself with this guide and its tables, you are ready to assimilate enough of a new culture to get you moving.

Everything you really need to know — from exchange rates and health tips to local customs and a brief historical overview — is at your fingertips, in a book that fits neatly in your jacket pocket.

If you don't know the territory — or the people — this guide is good company to any stranger in a strange land.

Patrick J. Leahy

U.S. Senator from Vermont

Appropriations Committee

Subcommittee on Foreign Operations

Special Merit Award

Vermont Book Professionals Association – Judged by
John Berry, Editor-in-Chief, *Library Journal*
Louise Berry, Director, **Darien** (Connecticut) **Library**

"The librarians we consulted instantly grabbed this for their travel collection. A mercifully light, handy guide, organized for both preparation and quick reference on site. Information on money, health, education, history, government, religion, a useful section on Spanish. and other crucial details for living in Mexico, all difficult to get at in other sources, are easy to find here."

About the Authors

Dr. Alvino E. Fantini and his wife, Beatriz Céspedes de Fantini, have been staff members of The Experiment in International Living since the mid-1960s. The Experiment is one of the oldest and most prestigious intercultural exchange organizations in the world. For nearly twenty years, the Fantinis ran a Mexican language and cultural orientation program for The Experiment at Oaxtepec, Tlaxcala, Valle de Bravo, and Metepec. This gave them a wonderful opportunity to explore Mexico, make hundreds of close Mexican friends, and follow their interests in anthropology, folk dancing, art, and Meso-American indigenous cultures (especially Aztec and Mayan).

When they are not visiting or teaching overseas, the Fantinis live in Vermont, where they are on the faculty of The School for International Training (SIT), which is the academic branch of World Learning, the parent organization of The U.S. Experiment.

At SIT, Beatriz Fantini directs the Language and Culture Center. Over the years, she has also taught Spanish and runs a remarkable variety of language and cultural orientation programs both in the United States and in several Latin American countries. She is a native of Bolivia.

Dr. Alvino Fantini is the director of Bilingual and Multicultural Education for the SIT Master of Arts in Teaching Program. Aside from his native English and Italian, he is fluent in Spanish and Portuguese and familiar with French, Greek, Esperanto, German, and Aymara. His Master's is in Latin American Studies and Anthropology, his Doctorate in Applied Linguistics, both from the University of Texas. For SIT and The Experiment, he has served as a director, teacher, consultant, translator, exchange leader, and materials developer for programs all over the world. Recently he served as president of SIETAR International (The Society for Intercultural Education, Training, and Research).

Between them, Dr. and Mrs. Fantini have written over fifty published books and articles on language and culture.

iv

Contents

3. Country Facts   40

4. The Spanish Language   65

Some Books about Mexico   89

1. First Steps

You are about to embark upon an adventure — living in another country. Your destination is Mexico. When you arrive, you will need to be able to satisfy some immediate survival needs. You will probably find that you must do some things differently from how you do them at home. This section is designed to help you get started learning how to live in Mexico. Although every town will be a little different, we can provide you with some basic facts about life in Mexico. Filling in the details will be up to you. So, while we can tell you, for instance, about restaurants and eating habits in Mexico, you will need to find places to eat that have food you like and can afford. And while we can tell you about different types of transportation in Mexico, you will still need to find the best way to get around the town where you live. We can suggest alternatives, but you will be making the final choices.

One final note: You may find that cultural changes, technological advances, and regional differences affect customs, values, systems, and even the "country facts" reported in this booklet. So "expect the unexpected," and be prepared to learn from your direct experience. The information in this section and those that follow should be used only as an initial guide. *¡Buena Suerte!*

This section covers the topics listed below. Read those of most interest to you now; you can read the others as the need arises.

1.1 Money
1.2 Food
1.3 Restaurants
1.4 Drinks and Drinking
1.5 Hotels
1.6 Tipping
1.7 Telephone
1.8 Letters, Telegrams, Faxes, and E-mail
1.9 Transportation
1.10 Shopping
1.11 Health and Medical Care
1.12 Bargaining
1.13 Electricity
1.14 Conversions

1.1 Money

The *peso* is the monetary unit used in Mexico. The symbol for it is $. The exchange value of the *peso* changes according to the world money market. The exchange rate has been quite stable in recent years at about 7 to 10 per $1 U.S. However, always check the official bank exchange rate before changing any significant amount of money.

The *peso* is available in 1, 2, 5, 10, and 20 *peso* coins and 20, 50, and 100 *peso* bills. It is divided into 100 *centavos*, and 5, 10, 20, and 50 *centavo* coins are in use. This is a simple and convenient system.

Banking hours in Mexico are often from 9:00 A.M. to 1:30 P.M., Monday through Friday. However, you can usually change money only until 1:00 P.M. Outside of Mexico City, banks may have special hours for exchanging money and traveler's cheeks. In the last few years, a variety of exchange houses, *cambios,* have come into being, and it is sometimes easier to change money through such establishments since there are many of them and they have longer hours. Both banks and *cambios* are closed on national holidays.

Traveler's checks are easy to change in large cities at hotels, shops, restaurants, and even in markets. In small towns it may be more difficult to use them. You can also change money at the airport and get a favorable exchange. The exchange rate may be less favorable in shops and restaurants. Your passport or other identification is normally required when changing traveler's checks.

Credit cards are accepted in many places and can also be used to get cash from automatic teller machines (*cajeros automáticos*). As in the U.S., these are becoming increasingly popular. Credit card charges and ATM withdrawals will be in *pesos* but billed to your account in U.S. dollars at the U.S. bank rate.

1.2 Food

Mexican cuisine is among the most exciting in the world. The Indian heritage and Spanish influence have combined to form a fantastic blend of colors and flavors. Don't be surprised if you find the food in Mexico much more varied and interesting than the Mexican food in U.S. restaurants and supermarkets.

In general, Mexican food is based on corn, rice, and beans. The staple of Mexican food is the *tortilla,* which is like a crepe made traditionally of corn flour. In many parts of Mexico, wheat *tortillas* are also common. A variety of dishes are based on the *tortilla.* Depending on how they are prepared (fried, rolled, etc.), the dishes change name. Some of the most popular *tortilla*-based dishes are: *enchiladas, tostadas tacos, flautas, chilaquiles, garnachas,* and *sopes.* Often, each region has a different name for the various shapes and contents of the *tortilla.* Corn flour is also used to make many other things, like *tamales,* which are made of corn dough with some type of stuffing and then wrapped in corn husks or banana leaves.

Next to *tortillas,* the most common starch in Mexico is rice. Mexicans do enjoy potatoes, pasta, and different kinds of breads and rolls, but rice cooked in a rich soup stock is eaten almost every day.

Mexicans commonly have *frijoles* (beans) in their daily diet. A dish of *frijoles* is usually served toward the end of the meal. There are several kinds of *frijoles* (black, red, white; small, medium, large), each with a different name. They are often served refried (*refritos*). Next to *frijoles* in importance, and with even more variety, are *chiles* (peppers). There are more than twenty kinds of *chiles* in Mexico. Some are mild; others are very hot. They are used in the preparation of different dishes, and the amount used varies from region to region. Not all Mexicans like fiery hot food, but many do.

Mexican food often uses many special ingredients and sauces. One special sauce is called *mole.* There are several varieties, the most famous being *mole poblano.* This is served only on special occasions since the preparation of the sauce is very elaborate. It is made with different types of *chiles*, many spices, and a mixture of almonds, peanuts, walnuts, chopped *tortillas*, tomatoes, and bittersweet chocolate. It is considered a specialty. Other *moles* are **pipián** (made with squash seeds called *pepitas*), **cacahuate mole** (made with peanuts), and others made with different types of *chiles*, vegetables, and spices.

Meat is frequently eaten by the middle and upper classes in Mexico whether in the form of a simple **burbacoa** (barbecue), **carnitas** (meat cooked until it shreds and comes apart), or pork in **adobe** (a mixture of *achiote*, a spice, and *chile*). Some special dishes combine various kinds of meats. **Pozole**, a dish originally from the state of Guerrero, is a delicious soup made with hulled corn, pork, chicken, and spare ribs, and then topped with oregano, radishes, shredded lettuce, and ground pepper.

Mexican cuisine boasts many regional specialities. Regional dishes are varied and use local produce and seasonings. In Veracruz and other coastal towns, for example, there is a variety of fish and seafood dishes, like **Huachinango a la veracruzana** (red snapper, Veracruz style), or *ceviche*. The first dish includes fish with a tomato-*chile* sauce, accompanied with green olives. The second is any kind of fish or seafood raw but marinated and served cold as an appetizer.

Because of Spanish influence, Mexicans are also quite fond of Spanish cuisine. Dishes such as **paella, gazpacho,** and **sopa de mariscos** appear in menus and in homes. Flan, also popular in Spain and most of Europe, is a caramel custard dessert available in most restaurants of any size in Mexico.

Some dishes that are typically thought of as "Mexican," like *chile con carne, burritos, nachos,* and *fajitas,* are actually more typical of the southwestern United States (Texas and New Mexico) , and they may not even be known in many areas of the country.

Finally, Mexicans have a great variety of wonderful fruits, local candies, and pastries which complement many of their meals. A list of items commonly found on Mexican menus appears in Chapter 4.

4

1.3 Restaurants

Depending on where you are in Mexico, you may find either a great variety of restaurants or just one or two local places. Mexico City has some of the best restaurants in the world. In addition to Mexican restaurants, there are those serving Italian, German, Japanese, Chinese, Swiss, and French cuisines.

Fine restaurants are found in the **Zona Rosa**, the expensive tourist district of Mexico City, and in Polanco and San Angel Pedregal. Mexican chain food restaurants are also scattered throughout the city, offering the famous *carnes al carbon* and *quesos fundidos* (charcoaled meat and melted cheese, served with wheat or corn flour *tortillas*). The best known Mexico City fast food chains are *Los Portales, El Potzocalli,* and *La Parrilla Suiza.* One can eat two *tacos* or a full **parrillada** (barbecue) accompanied by cold Mexican beer. Usually the menu is posted outside the restaurant, especially in the bigger restaurants. In Mexico you will also find some U.S.-style fast food establishments such as McDonalds, Aunt Jemima's, Burger Boy, VIPs, Denny's, and Pizza Hut.

Local restaurants in small towns tend to be family operations. Food is usually prepared for local taste, not for tourists. In some restaurants, you will find what is called **comida corrida,** which is the menu of the day offered for a fixed price. Usually it is quite economical and cheaper than ordering a meal *à la carte.*

A 10% value added tax (*Impuesto al Valor Adquirido*), identified by the initials **I.V.A.,** is added to the price of meals at the bottom of the bill. Tips are 10%–15% of the price of the meal (not including the I.V.A.), so an easy way to figure the amount of a tip is to give roughly the same amount as the tax.

Taco stands are found on many street corners in business districts. Like our hot dogs and hamburgers, they can be eaten at any time. Many stands also sell sandwiches and *tortas*. A **torta** is a sandwich made with a roll and filled with cooked or barbequed meats, ham, cheese, chicken, fritters, avocados, pork, veal cutlets, refried beans, or eggs. Other stands sell fresh fruit, sugar cane, pastries, and candies. In general, tourists who have not become accustomed to Mexican food are cautioned to avoid buying food from street vendors.

Mexican cuisine does not include many fresh vegetables. Vegetables are used in soups or arranged as garnish. Peppers are probably the most widely consumed vegetable. One specialty dish is **chiles rellenos** (a large green pepper, sometimes fairly hot, stuffed with cheese, dipped in a batter, and fried, then topped with tomato sauce.) During August, **chives en nogada** are in season, and they are a must. For this dish, *chiles* are stuffed with a mixture of minced beef and pork, with dried fruits and nuts. They are cooked and served cold, topped with a cream sauce made with ground walnuts and sprinkled with pomegranate seeds. This may be one of the most expensive dishes on the menu.

Aside from these basic foods, there are many specialties that require an educated taste. The famous *maguey* worms, corn fungus (*huitlacoche*), and zucchini flowers (fried, stewed, or in soup) are all specialties that one should try for a real Mexican experience.

1.4 Drinks and Drinking

Mexico has many regional drinks, both alcoholic and nonalcoholic. Most non-alcoholic drinks are fruit-based. The famous *licuados* are made from practically any fruit or vegetable. You can find, for example, a *licuado de zanahorias* (carrots) as well as one made with alfalfa. The most popular, however, are those made with fruit such as pineapple, melon, watermelon, peach, strawberries, and the many local fruits, such as *papaya, guanabana, zapote, tamarind,* and *guayaba.* All can be ordered with milk or water.

In Mexico, drinking the water has always been a "no-no" for both nationals and tourists. In general, tap water is avoided. Drinking water is usually boiled, filtered, or bottled. However, the word *agua* is used to define another popular beverage — a watered-down fruit juice. So, you might have an *agua de limón, agua de papaya, agua de sandía* (watermelon), etc., or another regional drink such as *horchata* (a rice drink). Mexicans also drink a lot of colas and other soft drinks.

At parties, family dinners, or visits to restaurants, young people (12+) are allowed to taste whatever is being served: *sangría,* beer, etc. It is normal for young people in Mexico to taste alcoholic beverages, and this is not seen as a problem. Beer is sold in most small stores, supermarkets, and sometimes department stores (*à la* K-mart). Although 18 is the official age limit in Mexico for drinking alcoholic beverages, it is not usually enforced.

Adults enjoy a great variety of excellent Mexican beers, and three very traditional alcoholic drinks of Indian origin, made from various types of cactus, are also popular. These are *mescal* from the *maguey* cactus and *pulque* and *tequila* from the *agave* cactus or century plant.

1.5 Hotels

Depending on where you are in Mexico, you will usually find a variety of hotels in at least two categories: the good and the not-so-good. Hotels are rated by stars; five stars are the very best. However, in small towns with only one or two hotels, this system does not apply. Local people are usually the best informants about hotel quality.

In larger cities, one can also find motels. However, lodgings labeled as motels are not necessarily nice places to stay. Although some hotels physically resemble an American "motel," they are still called hotels — this, despite the fact that you may park very close to your room.

When asking for a hotel room, be sure you request two double beds, two single beds, or whatever you wish. Unlike the United States, a double room does not necessarily have two twin beds. You should also be sure to inquire if there is hot water at all times. In larger cities, it is not usual to have specific hours for hot and cold water or to have the water turned off for several hours. In some towns, however, this is routine, especially in the dry season (October through May), when rain is scarce.

Most tourist areas in Mexico have an assortment of hotels. Low-priced hotels are certainly a bargain. However, just a little more money, you often can stay in a really nice place without overextending your budget.

1.6 Tipping

Tipping customs for restaurants have already been described. However, there are certain other services requiring tipping in Mexico that foreigners might not be aware of. For instance, gas station attendants get a tip, as do ushers in theaters and parking lot guards (including those who watch your car when it is parked at a meter on an open street). In general, anyone who provides a service gets a tip. Conversely, when you are a customer at the open market, you might get a "tip" from a vendor in the form of an extra apple, orange, or whatever fruit you are purchasing, especially if you are a good customer.

An institutionalized system of bribery is fairly common in Mexico. A sum of money may be given to guarantee a business deal, a purchase, or sometimes just a favor. There are many ways these transactions are hidden within the fairly corrupt system. These bribes may amount to thousands of dollars or, more commonly, just a few dollars when, for example, you are stopped by a traffic policeman. When bribes are offered to the police or other officials, such as inspectors, to avoid fines or delays, they are called *mordidas.* These are extremely common by North American standards, but they are usually offered in a discreet and diplomatic manner. The government is trying to discourage bribes to law enforcement personnel.

1.7 Telephone

There are coin-operated phones in most areas of Mexico. In big cities, they can be found on street corners and in shopping centers, restaurants, and other public places, although they may not be in working order. In small towns, pay telephones are less common. You may have to search for the *caseta de telefono* (phone booth or office). In very small towns, there may be only one central phone. To place a long distance call from a small town is not always quick or easy.

Because of inflation, it is difficult to say how much your call will cost. The airport in Mexico City has some free telephones for passengers and for anyone needing to make local calls from the airport. The Mexican phone system provides most of the services of phone companies in the U.S. You can place a *llamada por cobrar* (collect call) or *llamada con tarjeta de crédito* (credit card call), or, if you are going to reimburse the person whose telephone you are using, you might ask for a *llamada con tiempo y costo* (time and charges). The operators are quite good at making sure you have all the information you request.

The only frustrating part of using the phone may be getting an operator to answer the phone in the first place. The overseas line is often busy, but if you know the area code you can call long distance by direct dialing (known as *LADA*). Again, in some small towns, you may have problems getting the operator to accept your credit card; an operator may refuse to make your call. The tax for long distance calls may be as high as 40%. Because this tax is so high, it often makes sense to call collect if you are calling abroad, or, better yet, use a telephone credit card from your own country. In this case, use the number that allows you to dial direct to an operator within the U.S., and then place your call. You may also buy telephone cards in Mexico that can be used for both local and long-distance calls.

1.8 Letters, Telegrams, Faxes, and E-mail

Post offices in Mexico are usually open from 8:00 A.M. to 6:00 P.M. In large cities, the main post offices do not close at lunchtime; in small towns, they often close from 2:00 P.M. to 4:00 P.M. Post offices are also open on Saturday until 1:00 P.M.

Some places that sell postcards may also sell stamps, and then you only need to deposit the cards in the nearest mailbox. However, this is not advised since it may take some time before the boxes are emptied. If you are near a big hotel, use the hotel's mailbox, which is much more reliable.

The Mexican postal system is known to be slow even within the country. It is hard to predict when a letter will reach its destination. Letters to the U.S. from small towns in Mexico, for example, may take anywhere from a week to ten days, or even longer. A letter to Europe takes about the same amount of time. It is not advisable to send packages abroad from Mexico. In many cases, they don't reach their destination, and there is no way to guarantee their arrival.

Telegrams are sent from special telegraph offices often situated near the post office. It is easy to send telegrams, and — given the time it takes for a regular letter — many people opt for telegrams. There are also separate offices for sending cables or telex. As in the U.S., fax machines are becoming widely available, and faxes are the fastest way of sending a written message. Charges are often made both to send and to receive faxes. These are usually based on the number of pages, and the cost may be higher than in the U.S. Ask for the rates in advance.

E-mail is the fastest, easiest, and least expensive way to communicate if you have access to a computer and a way of getting on the Internet. As in cities all over the world, good hotels in Mexico are more and more likely to provide you with a way of getting on line in your room or in a business center. The best way to find out if this service is available wherever you are in Mexico is to ask.

1.9 Transportation

Mexico has two major airlines: *Mexicana* and *Aeroméxico.* They not only fly between major Mexican cities and the U.S. but also within Mexico itself. There are also smaller airlines.

The bus system in Mexico provides first-, second-, and third-class intercity travel. There are also luxury tourist buses that depart from the airport in Mexico City to several major cities and resorts. First-class buses also tend to go direct to their destination without making frequent stops as the second-class buses do. The higher the class, the cleaner, safer, and more comfortable the buses are. There are four major bus stations in Mexico City — north, east, south, and west. Each connects to different cities in different regions of the country. It is a good idea to purchase tickets in advance on first-class buses, where seats are numbered and reserved. This also avoids standing in long lines in a crowded bus station on the day of your trip. Tickets on other buses are normally sold only before boarding.

Mexico City has one of the best subway systems in Latin America. The subway is not only a very practical means of transportation, but an aesthetic experience as well. The stations are modern, often decorated with very artistic designs. The metro goes almost everywhere in the city. Bus stations often connect with the subway, so it is easy to arrive from an interior city to a bus station in the capital and then connect with a subway to the airport. Despite the fact that there are eight subway lines and several more under construction, the cars tend to be overcrowded.

Taxis range from inexpensive to expensive, depending on the city in Mexico. In large cities there may be taxis of various types. One type is called a *pesero* or *colectivo.* These travel only along a fixed route and pick up passengers until full. These used to cost a *peso* (hence their name), but now, with inflation, prices have gone up considerably, varying with the distance traveled.

Other taxis may or may not have meters. It is probably best to take only those with meters, since taxi drivers tend to make up rates on a whim, especially for foreigners. If you do take an unmetered taxi, be sure to negotiate the fare before you enter. Some taxis show price charts adjusting meter rates. It is sometimes difficult to get change for large bills, so be sure to carry enough small bills and change.

1.10 Shopping

Business hours change in Mexico according to the size of the city. In Mexico City, for example, there are stores that do not close at all for lunch. Others may close from 2:00 P.M. to 4:00 P.M. but will remain open until 9:00 P.M. In small towns, stores normally close from 2:00 to 4:00 P.M., and often you will not find anything open at these times. Even big department stores might close. Offices and some businesses that stay open all day will normally close at 7:00 P.M. instead of 9:00 P.M.

In Mexico City, you can find large commercial centers (shopping malls), and sometimes it is better to go to one of these in your area than to brave the traffic complications downtown. Some big department stores contain supermarkets. The tendency nowadays is a one-stop visit to avoid going from place to place. However, there are still various kinds of specialty stores (selling cold cuts, fish, cheese, etc.). One of the most common types of shops in Mexico is the *panadería* or *panificadora* (bakery). Since dinner is often a very light meal taken around 7:00 P.M. or later, Mexican families ohen opt for *pan dulce* (a sweet roll) and hot chocolate. Large *panaderías* may offer more than 100 varieties of sweet rolls. *Pan dulce* is also served with coffee in the morning, before or after the main part of breakfast (eggs, etc.).

There are many chain stores in Mexico. Some common ones are Gigante, Comercial Mexicana, Blanco, Aurrera, and, more recently, Wal-mart. They sell anything from cosmetics to food. Many big department store chains have several stores in Mexico City; these include Liverpool, París-Londres, Suburbia, and Sanborns (a source for English language books and periodicals). Most carry clothes and household items. American chains operating in Mexico City are Sears and Woolworth.

Aside from shops and stores, Mexico has many interesting and colorful open-air markets. In many towns, the market is a large, permanent structure. Other markets are held only on specific days, sometimes in one of the central squares of the town or village. They often start very early in the morning. This is a tradition that goes back to pre-Columbian times. In some towns, there are separate markets offering the arts and crafts of local artisans and offering food, clothing, and household wares. Both markets will be worth a visit. In parts of many cities, there are also less formal markets — areas where street peddlers set up stalls and sell all kinds of things. Other peddlers set up their stalls on street corners or at busy intersections where traffic has to stop for a stop light.

1.11 Bargaining

In Mexico, it is traditional to bargain. However, bargaining is not as common as it used to be. In large stores with cashiers, and in stores where prices are marked, you may not be able to bargain — unless, of course, the clerks feel they have had a bad day or think they may be able to sell you more if they bargain. In stores where the price is not marked, it is wise to bargain, because the price you are given probably reflects wishful thinking on the clerk's part. It is still common to bargain when buying at open-air markets and from street vendors.

© 1995 by Tatiana Parcero. Credit: Mexican Government Tourism Office.

Market scenes like this one are typical of the mercado or central market in almost every city and town in Mexico. Piles of brightly colored fresh fruits and vegetables in one stand. In the next, locally made candy, cooking and cleaning supplies, a butcher's stand where the meat is cut before your eyes to your specification, a stand for sewing supplies, school supplies, clothing, boots, or hats. On the other side, you might find a stand selling fresh fruit juices (jugos), fresh pastries, tamales, or tacos.

If an item is small and inexpensive, there may be no point in bargaining; your time may be worth more than the saving. However, if you are interested in a costly item, it is wise to check the price of the same item at several vendors to get a range of prices. Then offer half to two-thirds the asking price. Vendors will appear to be shocked and hurt, but they will generally offer a lower price. You, too, should look sorry, but you should raise your price only about as much as the vendors lowered theirs. If you don't want to buy an item, don't start bagaining. Once you come to an agreement, any vendor will expect you to buy. Most Mexicans enjoy bargaining. They will rarely be cross when you try, since this is a natural social exchange for them. If it is not part of your culture, don't feel embarrassed. Either pay too much — cheerfully — or relax and have fun bargaining. It is a wonderful way to practice your Spanish.

1.12 Health and Medical Care

Enjoying good health in Mexico requires common sense and a little specialized knowledge. Your frame of mind is important. Prepare yourself to make certain adjustments. Keep in mind that you are not accustomed to the food, water, and mode of life you will encounter, and that you must be moderate and cautious.

Take some precautions in trying new foods until you learn which ones agree with you. Go easy on hot sauces and highly seasoned foods until you become accustomed to them. You will want to try everything, but let yourself adjust gradually, eating only small portions in the beginning. During this adjustment phase, you'll want to show tact so your Mexican friends will understand that their food, though novel to you, is just as good as the food you eat at home. You must maintain a delicate balance between your good health and the diplomacy required when living in a Latin American environment.

Use good judgment. Remember that when you are in doubt about food or drink, as in all matters, it is wisest to err on the side of conservatism. Although unwashed, unclean fruit and vegetables can be dangerous — as they are in many parts of the world — the food is probably safe in better class Mexican restaurants. When in doubt, stick with peeled and cooked fruits and vegetables.

If you are at an altitude higher than that to which you are accustomed (perhaps in Mexico City), you may feel a bit uncomfortable, lethargic, and short of breath at first. Move more slowly and avoid extreme exercise. Soon you will adjust to the differences in air pressure and will be able to resume your normal pace. Remember that alcohol has a stronger effect at higher altitudes. The air pollution in Mexico City and other major cities also may affect your health unless you are accustomed to it at home. Again, take it easy.

To avoid fatigue and minor intestinal upsets, take advantage of the *siesta* when possible. Keep reasonable hours and get plenty of rest. Just in case the change of diet and other factors (chemical content of the water, overtiredness, nervousness, etc.)

should cause diarrhea, you will find effective remedies in drug-stores. Also drink herbal teas (like *manzanilla* or chamomile), and eat boiled rice, very ripe bananas, and other constipants. Dry toast and plain boiled chicken from which all fat has been removed may be taken for nourishment. If you have a fever or if these treatments are not effective, contact a doctor immediately.

One of the most common problems that tourists to Mexico experience is "soft stool," not to be confused with diarrhea. Soft stool is often caused by the change of diet and increase in con-sumption of fresh fruits, especially *mango* and *papaya*, whereas diarrhea may be an indication of an infection or a drastic change of diet.

Tap water is not always safe in Mexico. *It is advisable not to drink tap water under any circumstances, even in big cities.* Mexicans buy water sold in 10 gallon bottles, and they are care-ful about not drinking water from the tap. Most homes have pu-rified or boiled, filtered, or bottled water. Mineral water is very common in Mexico. Hotels and restaurants always use bottled water, with or without "gas" (carbonation) or water that has been specially filtered. Even so, depending on where you are, when you order a drink, you might want to skip the ice. Also, take care to avoid tap water and use bottled water even when brushing your teeth.

The Mexican government provides extensive medical care through the social security system, which operates hospitals and clinics all over the country. For those who are members of this system, medical service and medicines are provided free of charge. Naturally, private doctors and hospitals are also available. In many cases, however, the experiences of the people you are stay-ing or working with may provide the most effective treatments for many problems you may encounter. The Mexican government is also opening 12 bilingual medical centers in major tourist ar-eas. These will operate 24 hours a day and will work in conjunc-tion with several medical centers in the U.S.

1.13 Electricity

The current in Mexico is normally 110–115 volts. However, there are a few places where 200–220 voltage is still in use. Three-pronged outlets are not common in Mexico, not even for large machines.

1.14 Conversions

Depending on what you are measuring or weighing, systems vary in Mexico. In most cases, the metric system is the common practice. In liquid measurements, however, the gallon system (fluid ounces) is sometimes used. The following charts are provided to help you make the necessary conversions.

Measurements

Metric	U.S.
Weights and Linear	
1 gram (g)	0.035 ounce
454 grams	1 pound
1 kilogram ("kilo")	2.2 pounds
1 centimeter (cm)	0.3937 inch
2.54 centimeters	1 inch
1 meter (m)	3.280 feet
1609.3 meters	1 mile
Liquid Measure	
l liter (l)	2.113 pints
l liter	1.056 quarts
3.785 liter	1 gallon
Dry Measure	
l liter	0.908 quart
1 dekaliter (10 liters)	1.135 pecks
1 hectoliter (100 liters)	2.837 bushels

Metric		U.S.	
	Kitchen Equivalents		
200 grams		1 cup sugar	
150 g		1 cup flour	
5 g		1 teaspoon	
12 g		1 tablespoon	

Kilometers and Miles

1 km	0.62 mile	25 km	15.5 mile
3	1.8	35	21.7
5	3.1	50	31.0
8	4.9	100	62.1
10	6.2	200	124.2
15	9.3	300	186.4
20	12.4	500	310.6

Thermometer Readings*

38°C	100.4°F	0°C	32°F
35°	95°	–5°	23°
30°	86°	–10°	14°
25°	77°	–15°	5°
20°	68°	–17.77°	0°
10°	50°	–25°	–13°
5°	41°	–30°	–22°

*Mexican thermometers use the centigrade scale. To convert Fahrenheit to centigrade, subtract 32, then multiply by 5 and divide by 9. To convert centigrade to Fahrenheit, multiply by 9, divide by 5 and add 32. For example, 21°C = 69.8°F precisely. The chart above gives an approximate conversion.

If you don't have a calculator handy or don't have time for longhand calculations, this very rough rule of thumb will give you the approximate Fahrenheit equivalent of centigrade temperatures: The centigrade temperature times two plus 30 equals the approximate Fahrenheit, or C° x 2 + 30 = F° (approx.).

Clothing Sizes

Skirts, Dresses, Coats		*Blouses*	
Mexico	**U.S.**	**Mexico**	**U.S.**
38	10	30	30
40	12	32	32
42	14	34	34
44	16	36	36
46	18	38	38
48	20	40	40

Shirts		*Shoes*	
Mexico	U.S.	Mexico	U.S.
36	14	3	5
37	14 1/2	4	6
38	15	5	7
39	15 1/2	6	8

2. Customs and Values

Now that you have a handle on some basic facts about where to find what you need and how to get it, you will want to begin looking more closely at how people live in Mexico. Since Mexicans are to be your new friends and family, it is important to understand their customs and values so that you can fit into their world successfully. The topics covered in this section have been chosen to help you begin your study of Mexican customs and values. Again, it will be up to you to learn the specifics about the people with whom you live and interact. The information we give you here is only a place for you to start. This is a beginning for your cultural exploration; it will be up to you to complete it.

The following topics are covered in this section:

2.1 Greetings and Leave-takings

Mexicans take a lot of time for greetings and leave-takings. Depending on the time of day, when seeing someone for the first time, they may greet people with either **"Buenos días"** (from early morning to noon), **"Buenas tardes"** (from noon to twilight, about 6:00 or 7:00 P.M.), or **"Buenas noches"** (from twilight on). It is customary to respond in the same manner, responding *"Buenos días,"* for example, in the morning. Mexicans also use several less formal expressions that are equivalent to "Hi," "How are you?" "What's happening?" (**"Hola," "¿Qué tal?" "¿Qué hubo?" "¿Cómo te va?" "¿Qué onda?"**). This last expression is more common among young people.

When Mexicans pass in the street and don't stop to talk, they nod, smile, and say, **"Adios"** ("Goodbye") This may seem very odd at first, but it is at least as logical as greeting someone you don't plan to talk to.

Mexicans will most often shake hands when meeting someone for the first time. Young people, particularly men, continue this tradition, although women also shake hands. Mexicans don't often include names in introductions. Rather, they present the person as "a friend," and it is expected that the friend will inject his or her name. It is not a matter of being impolite or being slighted. The most common response when being introduced is **"Mucho gusto,"** to which one answers, *"Mucho gusto,"* or **"Igualmente."** Young people may use the more informal **"Hola."**

Leave-taking expressions depend on whether you are going to see the person later or not, and indicate the degree of certainty ranging from **"Hasta luego"** or **"Hasta pronto"** to **"Adiós."**

2.2 Titles

Titles based on social class or status are rare in Mexico. However, titles based on occupation, such as *senador* (senator), *gobernador* (governor), *alcalde* (mayor), or *padre* (priest), are used frequently. *Doctor* is often used, not only for a medical doctor, but for lawyers and professors as well. A commonly used title, and one that carries a lot of weight in Mexico, is *licenciado(a)* (university graduate). Calling elderly people *Don* or *Doña* is another way to show respect.

The most widely used titles are those that express marital status. They are *señor* (Mr.), *señora* (Mrs.), and *señorita* (Miss). There is no equivalent to "Ms." in Mexico. When in doubt, if the woman is young, Mexicans will generally say "*señorita*."

Finally, although "American" is not a title, it is important to note that Mexicans and most other Latin Americans normally refer to people from the U.S. and Canada as *norteamericanos* (North Americans). They consider themselves and everyone else from anywhere in the Americas to be "Americans," and some Mexicans resent the way the term is used in the U.S. Since this can be a delicate and sensitive point, it is best to introduce yourself as a North American or to say that you are from the U.S. or Canada.

2.3 Conversation Topics

Mexicans often show a great deal of interest in foreign visitors. These visitors may find themselves besieged by questions. Many of these questions may be based on preconceived ideas about foreigners. For example, you might be asked how many cars your family owns, the assumption being that everyone in the U.S. owns his or her own car. Mexicans are very open. Sometimes people feel that they are overly curious, but they are simply taking a special interest in people.

Most Mexicans are "people" people. They like small talk, and sometimes foreigners get impatient with what they consider to be a lack of depth in their conversations. In a business situation, for example, Americans are more likely to want to get down to business.

Mexico, like most of Latin America, is a "polychronic" society, as is most of Latin America. This means that people often speak together at the same time. At the dinner table, for example, everyone may be talking at the same time, with the same intensity and volume! This may take some getting used to. In Mexican culture, everyone has a chance to participate, and nearly everyone does. One Mexican conversational trait is to agree ostensibly, but not really. Thus, you might be told one thing, and then it might seem that the Mexicans you are talking to have suddenly changed their opinion. This does not mean that they are hypocritical; rather, it shows they are considerate of those to whom they are talking. They are being diplomatic; they don't wish to offend. They may say one thing to intimate friends and something different — perhaps the exact opposite of what they've just said — to others.

2.4 Friendship

Mexicans are known for being warm, open people. They sometimes call people *amigo* to be friendly, but without really meaning that they feel close. For example, a casual acquaintance may be called *amigo,* and vendors often call foreign customers *amigo* as part of their sales pitch. On the other hand, true friendships are very important to Mexicans. They are very loyal people and are always willing to do anything for a friend. In the beginning of a friendship, they may be as open as North Americans — open on the surface. However, they soon go beyond that and can quickly become very involved and remain very close to their friends. They are affectionate and not shy about expressing their feelings toward each other.

Mexicans develop true, long-lasting friendships. This is possible because Mexicans have not until recently been a mobile society; they have tended to stay in their home communities for their entire lives, and they still like to be surrounded by those who are close to them.

2.5 Gender Relations

As they are everywhere in the world, relations between women and men are changing in Mexico. One can't make a generalization about these changes that will fit all of Mexico or all Mexicans, because there are areas that are more traditional and conservative and other areas, like Mexico City, where change is happening rapidly. The relations between specific men and women are, of course, personal and individual. They are determined by many social, educational, and cultural factors. Generalizations can be helpful, however, if you recognize their limitations and make a point of observing people in the part of Mexico where you are.

Here are a few generalizations about good manners that will hold true in most of Mexico today. Fifty years ago, these were true throughout North America, but the feminist movement discouraged such manners, feeling that they were demeaning to women. In Mexico, however, these manners are still expected. Men are expected to open doors for women and to allow them to pass first. If a man and a woman meet so that they might run into one another — say at a narrow place in a sidewalk — the man will step aside and let the woman pass. If they are walking down a street together, the man will walk on the outside, closest to the street. When getting on or off a bus, a man will always let a woman go first, and he will generally offer his seat to a woman who is standing.

Generally, it is considered rude for men to sit at a social gathering while women are standing. If a woman arrives at a party where all the chairs are taken, men will scramble to find another chair or to offer her their own. When a woman comes up to a table, all the men will stand up to greet her and remain standing until she either sits or leaves. If a man invites a woman out to dinner, he will expect to pull out her chair for her when she sits down and to pay for them both.

To some North Americans and Europeans, these manners seem old-fashioned and sexist. But in Mexico, both men and women expect everyone to behave in this way. It is simply considered to be polite. Men give way to women politely, and women accept it with a polite smile and *"gracias."* Most Mexicans take it in their stride when foreigners are pushy and rude, but good manners as they understand them are appreciated.

These manners have deep cultural roots and, as a result, have not changed for most Mexicans even under the influence of North American television and movies and the constant mixing of cultures in the border states. Mexican women are often strong, intelligent, and independent, but they are still protected and treated with deference by most Mexican men, and they accept it. Men often have a similar split in their relations with women. They may see themselves as being respectful and protective, while at the same time they are *macho* and aggressive. These apparent contradictions are typical of Mexican gender relations, though certainly not universal. The roles of men and women in the home, workplace, and community vary widely and are changing. Cultural changes provoke strong reactions in Mexico as they do everywhere. Perhaps the best way to make a general statement about Mexican gender relations at this time is to say that they are conservative but unsettled.

2.6 Invitations

Mexicans are often informal; extending "open invitations" is a common practice. This invitation is generally more serious than the North American "Come and visit anytime." Mexicans don't really expect that you will drop in, but they'll be pleased when you do. They like to pay impromptu visits to friends and relatives without calling first and making arrangements. A Mexican household is an open place. Children as well as adults visit each other freely. However, this openness is limited to friends and family; uninvited acquaintances and strangers are not generally brought into the home when they call. Don't be insulted if you are left waiting at the door when you stop to see someone you don't know.

If you are invited to a dinner or to a party, you are not expected to bring anything. As a courtesy, however, you may take flowers, chocolates, or a small gift. A souvenir from your own city, state, or country would be appreciated and appropriate.

Written invitations don't have to be answered as soon as is customary in the States. If the invitation is to a formal affair, you are expected to respond by the requested date. Most dance parties are by open invitation and are quite casual. A dance party might be scheduled to start at 9:00 P.M., but people will not be expected to arrive before 10:00 P.M. or later. Mexicans are also very informal about allowing people to bring friends. In small towns, everyone usually knows everyone else. Bringing friends is customary, although it might be considered rude of a foreigner to bring strangers to a party.

When Mexicans go out in a group, each person pays their own expenses. However, sometimes the person who suggested going out may expect to pay, particularly if the group are all of the same gender. If a man invites a woman out, he expects to pay. Not to do so would be considered rude. Because you are a foreigner, Mexicans may feel obligated to pay for you, to be hospitable. Young people often tease North Americans by suggesting that because they have dollars, they should pay; but they are really joking. When you are treated by someone, however, it is appropriate to reciprocate at some other time.

2.7 Personal Space and Privacy

The concepts of personal space, privacy, and being alone are foreign to Mexicans. They are gregarious people and like to be surrounded by family and friends. They enjoy one another's company even when verbal interaction is kept to a minimum. In contrast to many other cultures, Mexicans are used to touching each other quite often. For example, when they are conversing, they might put a hand on your shoulder. While walking down the street, they might take your arm. In greeting each other, the intensity of touching varies from a strong handshake to a very Mexican *abrazo* (hug). They stand close when talking to one another. In public transportation, they are not offended if another passenger is so close that they rub shoulders or hips. People who are not used to such physical contact might accuse Mexicans of getting too close. However, they are simply behaving in the same manner as they would with other Mexicans. Of course, physical contact with the opposite sex is another matter and may be misunderstood.

2.8 Time

Time is not always "of the essence" in Mexico. People are very casual about the hour of a doctor's appointment, a business call, a visit to a friend, a party, or an official event. It has been said that the only events that start on time in Mexico are the bullfights and Mass. Events with fixed schedules, like movies, ballets, and theater, do start on time, or no more than 5 to 20 minutes late. But other than these exceptions, being on time in general is not a major concern. This is often frustrating for foreigners.

2.9 Silence

Mexican people are used to noise. When they turn on a TV, radio, tape machine, or CD player, the volume always seems to be too high for foreigners. In the States, people usually don't talk in the waiting room of a doctor's office. In fact, doctors keep a supply of magazines for their patients to read. In Mexico, people engage freely in conversation with other patients. Every patient gets to hear about someone else's illnesses. It is also common for people to start talking to complete strangers on buses or while waiting in a line. Silence is rarely kept. Even at the movies, which are often subtitled, people will start talking, especially when they are reading the subtitles out loud rather than listening to the sound.

2.10 Equality

Some Mexicans are very proud of their Indian heritage; others are proud of their Hispanic blood. Most Mexicans give their racial inheritance little thought. This racial consciousness varies, of course, depending on the person's age, locale, and economic and social class. Over the centuries, and particularly since the Revolution, Mexico has integrated the Indian population magnificently. In fact, the percentage of Mexicans of "pure" European ancestry is relatively small. By far the largest ethnic group is the *mestizos* ("mixed blood"), then the Indians, and then those of European (mostly Spanish) descent. There are also small numbers of Asians and people of other ethnic groups. No matter what a person's background, when it comes to positions in government or private enterprise, qualifications are what count. Most Mexicans are very proud of their *mestizo* nation with its rich cultural diversity. At the same time, Mexicans find blondes very attractive. Many ads feature blondes, and young people with bleached blond hair are not uncommon.

Socially, however, there are class distinctions. For example, upper-class Mexicans (business people or professionals) and service workers (such as maids, taxi drivers, or waiters) do not usually associate socially. They may be very friendly on a casual basis, but they keep their distance because they have been brought up that way. In general, Mexicans are quite class conscious.

2.11 Belonging to a Group

The concept of "doing your own thing" is foreign to Mexicans. Those who always or occasionally do their own thing are not always popular members of their community. They are regarded as *raros* (strange) or sometimes as "liberals."

Most Mexicans, particularly in small towns, conform very much to the rules society outlines for them. Nonconformity is not seen as a positive quality. The family structure validates and reinforces this conformity. Children are brought up with the custom of obeying both people and rules. Consequently, families don't often experience the generation gap between children and parents that seems to prevail elsewhere.

Mexicans' openness is probably best conveyed through the phrase *"Estás en tu casa"* ("My home is your home" / "You are in your house"). This expression refers not only to the physical structure of the home, but also to the customs, values, attitudes, and everything else that goes along with being in a Mexican home.

2.12 Eating Customs and Meals

Mexicans enjoy spending time together at the table, eating and talking, whenever possible. When the meal is over, the family typically lingers at the table and continues the conversation. This is especially true in families that have a maid. Maids are very common in Mexico, and not just among wealthy families. They are typically referred to as *la muchacha,* particularly when they are young.

Mexican table manners dictate that you may eat with either hand, left or right, but that the hand you are not using must remain on the table, not in your lap. When you have finished, both hands remain on the table.

Many Mexican dishes are typically eaten using your hands and a *tortilla* instead of knives and forks. However, if this makes you uncomfortable, it is perfectly appropriate to ask for a fork.

In the U.S., talking with your mouth full and burping at the table are considered to be bad table manners. You will probably notice that Mexicans sometimes speak while eating. This is not always true, but it is a general pattern. However, they never burp at the table or anywhere else in the presence of others. In a very informal situation, it sometimes happens, but it is considered ill mannered.

When offered more to eat, it is common to say **"No, gracias"** the first time but to accept the second or third time food is offered. This is a common practice. Even if you say "No" firmly, your hosts will continue to offer, thinking that you are simply following their custom. They are being polite in encouraging you. In response, it is polite to be patient, compliment the food, but not take more than you want.

Although Mexicans eat three meals a day, they seem to eat even more often because snacks (**antojitos**) are common. The principal meals are breakfast (**desayuno**), lunch (**comida**), and dinner (**cena**). *Desayuno* is often a substantial amount of food, consisting of juice, sweet rolls, eggs, toast or *tortillas,* and coffee. However, sometimes one has a *desayuno* consisting of only coffee and sweet rolls followed a few hours later by **almuerzo** (akin to brunch). Sometimes this includes dishes made with *tortillas, chiles,* and tomatoes, or with meat and beans.

Lunch (*comida*) is the main meal in Mexico, and it usually takes place between 2:00 P.M. and 4:00 P.M. This meal often takes a long time, and the time they finish determines whether they have an evening meal or not. A *comida* usually ends with a dish of *frijoles,* followed by fruit or dessert and coffee. (See the note at the end of this chapter.)

Dinner (*cena*) varies. If it is a formal dinner, it might begin quite late. At home, however, most people usually eat a light meal at 7:00 P.M. or later. This may consist of only chocolate and sweet rolls. However, housewives also like to use leftovers from the afternoon dinner for this meal.

Mexicans snack frequently, seemingly at any time — in the midmorning and mid-evening, as well as late at night. If they are out on the street, they may have one of the many *antojitos mexicanos* (*quesadillas, tacos,* etc.).

2.13 Family Life

It is difficult to generalize about family life in Mexico because so much depends on the social class and economic status of the family. However, there are some basic characteristics that can be cited as fairly general.

Typically, the family unit is very tight. Because Mexico's society is not a mobile one, families tend to live in close proximity, and the family unit remains central throughout people's lives. The Mexican extended family consists of aunts, uncles, cousins, grandparents, and even godparents (***padrinos***).

Elderly people are shown a lot of respect. It is uncommon for old people to be placed in nursing homes; to do so might be considered an indication that their children did not care about their happiness. When older persons cannot live alone, they usually live with their children and their children's families. The opinions of older people are very much respected in most homes, and they provide a lot of guidance for the extended family.

Children, especially girls, are expected to live with their parents until they get married. Even children who go to college don't always move out of the house since they rarely pick a college that is out of town. Even after marriage, in some cases, children may bring their spouses home to live with their parents. This practice, however, is disappearing. To find work, more and more children need to move, often to the big cities or to other sections of the city near their work.

If they are living outside of the home, married children usually keep in close touch with their parents, often on a daily basis. However, this practice is also changing in larger cities. Today, increased numbers of middle-class Mexican women work outside the home, so that daily contact with their extended families is reserved increasingly for Sundays and holidays.

Children tend to choose a career that allows them to follow the family profession or business. For example, in many families it is common to find three generations of dentists, lawyers, or doctors, and they keep the same name professionally.

Within the family, as well as within society, distinctions between male and female roles are very marked. Although there have been slight changes in this respect, these roles are still deeply ingrained. Mexican men have been classified as *"machistas."* Women, though equal citizens under the law, often don't have the same opportunities as men. The traditional role of the Mexican women is still that of taking care of the house and children. Even though many more women are now either pursuing professional interests or are going out to earn money in shops, factories, or other people's homes to help make ends meet, there are still many small towns and provincial cities in which the older values and traditions prevail and women stay home.

In general, Mexican men do not expect to do housework. Children, no matter their age, don't do many chores either. Housework is shared among the women of the family or between the wife and servants — housekeepers, cooks, and maids.

Both people's individual names and their family names are very important. Because families are so close and because they often remain in the same geographical area, they sometimes build reputations based on their names. Therefore, as in the Spanish tradition, an individual's name may indicate not only his or her family but also his or her place in society. The naming system is as follows:

(husband)	Jose **Fernández** Flores
(wife)	Elena Rojas de **Fernández** F.
(son)	Pedro **Fernández** Flores
(daughter)	Elena **Fernández** Rojas
(married daughter)	Teresa **Fernández** de González
(son-in-law)	Jesús González Burgos

2.14 Leisure

Mexicans en joy leisure time in a variety of ways. In sports, soccer (called *fútbol* in Spanish) is very popular. From their earliest years, children learn to kick a soccer ball. This becomes so ingrained that you can often see children kicking stones or any objects they encounter as they walk down the street. The other great passion for sports-minded Mexicans is baseball, both as a participant and as a spectator sport.

Both men and women enjoy tennis, golf, swimming, volleyball, and basketball, which they might play depending, in great part, on their social class. Racquetball and *jai-alai* are also played but are popular mostly among men of the upper class. Jogging has also become common in recent years, although in more provincial towns, joggers may still be a rare sight.

Bullfights are a popular leisure-time activity for many Mexicans. A few participate, taking some role in the  drama, but most go to the bullring to enjoy the music and the great traditional pageant of life and death.

Mexico offers many vacation options. In and around most Mexican cities and towns, there are public parks where people enjoy picnics, informal sports, and just relaxing for the day outdoors. The Mexican Social Security System operates various vacation centers, available to individuals who pay into this system. These centers are quite large and have all kinds of facilities. Although they are concentrated in only certain sections of the country, other privately owned *balnearios* (resorts) for vacationers are found in many areas. And, of course, Mexico's many splendid beach resorts are draw both Mexican and foreign vacationers, particularly over holidays.

Mexicans also like to visit their numerous historical and archaeological sites. Especially on Sundays and holidays, people enjoy visiting museums and the numerous archaeological zones representing their grand Indian heritage.

Television takes up a lot of free time in Mexico. This is especially true in small towns. Major soap operas are of national importance, and the latest episodes are commonly discussed among many individuals.

Movies are also popular in Mexico. Movie theaters are full, especially on Saturday and Sunday. It seems that weekends are mainly devoted to sports during the day and movies at night.

Mexicans read a lot, whether it is newspapers, magazines, novels, or comic books. There is a great demand for magazines, and they exist in great numbers. A favorite reading form is the "photo-novel" (*fotonovela*). These publications are short stories, often romances, printed with photographs in a comic book format.

2.15 Holiday Celebrations

Many holidays are celebrated in Mexico. Most are either of a patriotic or religious nature. Some national patriotic holidays are February 5th (Anniversary of the Constitution), September 16th (Independence Day), and November 20th (Anniversary of the Revolution). Others of lesser importance are also celebrated more or less elaborately according to the area. The March 21st birthday of Benito Juárez (a famous president of Indian origin and a contemporary of Abraham Lincoln) is an example.

Of the religious holidays, perhaps the most elaborate is the Christmas season. A Mexican celebration of Christmas starts nine days before Christmas Day. This period is called *posadas,* which is a re-enactment of the journey made by Joseph and Mary in search of a place to stay. Each night throughout this time, groups of friends go from house to house singing traditional songs, ending with the traditional *piñata.*

On the last night of *posadas,* which is Christmas Eve, the celebration is much more sedate. Both Christmas and New Year's Eve are family celebrations. Sometimes younger adults in the family may attend parties and the older members stay at home. Usually the grandparents' or some other family member's home is large enough to accommodate a large group.

 Another important celebration of both religious and pagan origin is *Carnival*. It takes place just before the Lenten season begins, 40 days before Easter Sunday. The celebration varies from city to city. In some areas there is no *Carnival* celebration at all, whereas in other areas, notably Mazatlán and Veracruz, the celebration includes parades, contests, costumes, etc., over several days and is organized with the support of the state government.

Holy Week (Palm Sunday through Easter Sunday) is both a period of religious celebration and an opportunity for at least a long weekend. Many people leave their own city to go to a vacation spot, often one of the coastal areas. This provides a chance to get away from both one's job and home routine.

The *Virgin of Guadalupe* enjoys a special day on the Mexican calendar. Her feast day is December 12th. Although it is not a federal holiday, it is still widely observed; the banks are closed. Mexicans are also accustomed to celebrating their own saint's days (i.e., the day of the saint after whom they are named). Some saint's days are celebrated more than others. Particularly popular celebrations are saints Juan, Pedro, Pablo, Concepción, and Guadalupe. It is less common for people to celebrate their birthday than their saint's day.

Thanksgiving and St. Patrick's Day are not known to most Mexicans. However, *St. Valentine's Day* is becoming popular as a celebration of friendship. A celebration similar to Halloween is a long-standing tradition in Mexico. The *Day of the Dead*, like Halloween, is celebrated on the night before the church commemoration of All Souls' Day (All Saints' Day) at the end of October. This is an important religious celebration in Mexico, and in some towns there are special traditional observances, including a graveyard vigil, folkloric candy skulls, toy coffins, firecrackers, colorful papier-mâché figures, and marigolds, the sacred flower of the dead in Aztec culture. As with Halloween, stores are full of these things for weeks before the holiday.

In general, Mexicans like parties and celebrations. They always seem to find reasons to have a party, and they enjoy both traditional and popular music, lots of people, lots of noise, food, etc. Practically anything can provide a reason for a party — a birth, a christening, a birthday or saint's day, a farewell. Sometimes small social gatherings evolve into a dance party that might last until the early morning hours. Food might be served when the party is over, or friends may go out to the street to find one of the all-night restaurants where they can top off the festivities with *pozole* or a dish of spicy *menudo* (tripe in a hot sauce).

2.16 Culture Bumps

Contact with people from another culture, whether in your own country or abroad, inevitably produces surprises — some pleasant, some not. These result from differences, particularly in language, values, and behaviors. Although we know other cultures are different, it is another thing to experience and to deal with the differences. While it is easy to accept pleasant surprises, the same is not true for unpleasant ones. The differences that cause irritations ranging from minor to serious are called "culture bumps."

In Mexico, culture bumps may occur in a number of areas. Clearly the more you know about the local culture, the less likely you are to be in conflict with it. However, if you are new to the culture, it is best to anticipate that problems will arise. These can range from simple matters of daily life, such as how to walk down a busy street, to more important matters such as gender relations. Coping with these culture bumps is part of living in Mexico, and in the experience of coping you will have opportunities to learn about both Mexican culture and your own. This is one of the reasons the intercultural experience usually results in deepening your self-awareness while you are also developing new knowledge, skills, and attitudes (hopefully positive ones).

Many North Americans have cited as personal culture bumps things like these:

- *The noise level:* Mexicans generally tolerate more noise than North Americans. For example, it is not unusual for drivers to use their horns a lot, for loudspeakers to be *really* loud (even on public buses), for people to talk during concerts and movies, and for children to be allowed to scream in public places.
- *The sense of time:* Mexicans are unpredictable about time. They are often late, and they show no remorse about it. Why? They don't have the same sense that they need to be "on time."
- *Walking down the street:* Mexicans don't follow any pattern while walking. For example, people walk on either side of streets or sidewalks in either direction, and there is no tradition of passing people you meet on the left or right. You also have to keep your eyes open for hazards in streets and sidewalks that make it difficult to pass — a missing grate, a hole, or a vendor's stand.
- *The need to please:* Mexicans typically tell you what they think you want to hear. For example, if you say you would like to go to the beach, your friend will say they would love to take you — and they really would, although they know they probably can't. If you ask someone how to get to the folk art museum, they may tell you — even though they really have no idea. They just don't want to disappoint you by saying they can't help you.
- *Cleaning up:* Mexican homes are generally very neat and clean. In fact, the floors are often swept and washed every day. But outside, in the garden or in the street, the picture is different. Many Mexicans are unconcerned about littering, Europeans and North Americans who feel strongly about picking up litter find this difficult to adjust to.
- *Anti-U.S. feelings among your friends:* Mexicans are often nationalistic and quite proud of their country. Because the U.S. has overpowered Mexico politically and militarily several times in the past, and because Mexicans are aware that some North Americans are condescending toward Mexico, some Mexicans distrust and dislike the U.S. government, although this rarely means they are prejudiced against individual North Americans. It is quite common to see anti-U.S. car-

toons and news items in the papers, but that doesn't mean that the person reading the paper won't accept you as an individual.

- *Use of public space:* Mexicans typically make themselves at home in public places. For example, it is more common in Mexico than in the U.S. or Canada to see people sleeping, eating, or embracing and kissing in public. People will sit or squat down on curbs and sidewalks or in entryways, and one often sees people taking naps in parks or any green space.
- *Power and privilege:* Mexicans are more comfortable showing their financial, social, and political status than most other North Americans. For example, they may quite openly use their status or personal connections to obtain personal favors or exemptions.
- *Getting change for big bills:* You may end up paying too much unless you carry small bills. For example, taxi drivers often can't or won't make change, and shop owners commonly decline to change a big bill for you unless you are buying something.

Most of these examples seem quite innocuous when read, but they can be irritating when experienced. You expect simple things to happen they way they do in your home country. When they don't, the normal reaction is to get mad at an individual or to be annoyed at the culture.

The trick to avoiding this negative experience is to know what your host Mexicans expect in the Mexican situation. You can't avoid the culture bumps; they are part of any intercultural experience. However, knowing about these culture bumps ahead of time will help you anticipate and avoid the pain, and it may also make you more open to discovering other culture bumps of your own once you are in Mexico. How you deal with them will serve as an indicator of your level of adjustment. You must make your own decisions about whether to be annoyed or to accept the difference between your way and the new way — the Mexican way.

A Note on the Generalizations in This Chapter

The observations on Mexican customs and values in this chapter are generally true of traditional Mexican society. However, the last few years have brought many changes. Some are particularly apparent in the industrialized North, where the effect of U.S. customs and values is as strong as the effect of Mexican customs and values is in the American Southwest. Other changes are more apparent in Mexico City. For example, people who commute to work for two or three hours across what is now the largest city in the Americas, if not in the world, do not run home for the midday meal. Furthermore, although Mexicans have traditionally tended to stay in their native hometowns, today there are millions of people who have uprooted themselves to look for work in Mexico City, Guadalajara, and other big cities. All this has had a profound effect on Mexican culture. So take these generalizations with a grain of salt, and contrast them with what you find in reality in Mexico.

3. Country Facts

As you become more comfortable living in Mexico, you will find that you want to know more facts about the country; for example, how it is organized and governed, etc. This section consists of the following sub jects:

3.1 History
3.2 Map: Cities of Mexico
3.3 People
3.4 Land and Climate (with map)
3.5 Government
3.6 Economy
3.7 Education
3.8 Religion
3.9 Arts

3.1 History

Mexico has a rich and complex history. The Mexican people, in general, are fascinated by it and feel strongly that their past is important to their national identity. This is particularly true of the pre-Colonial period. Since the Revolution of 1920, the government has focused popular interest on the succession of advanced Mexican Indian civilizations that flourished before the coming of Cortés and the Conquest (1521). These cultures were in many ways as impressive as their contemporaries in Europe and Asia. It does not diminish the importance of the Mayas, the Toltecs, or the Aztecs to point out the important fact that today's Mexican civilization is not only Indian but also very Spanish; it is a *mestizo* or mixed culture.

The love of this *mestizo* culture for its pre-Hispanic past is very widespread and significant, as is the way it ignores its Spanish roots. This is an overstatement, but the phenomenon is interesting. Images of ancient Mexico are seen everywhere. For example, Cuauhtémoc, the last Aztec emperor, whose brief reign ended in disaster because he resisted the conquest, is a great national hero. Mexicans are proud that the basics of Indian food (corn, beans, tomatoes, *chiles*, avocados, and chocolate) are still the basis of typical Mexican cooking. By contrast, they say little about Spanish culture. They take for granted the wheat and rice, the oranges, lemons, bananas, and sugar; the meat of domesticated animals they eat every day; the wheel; the colonial architecture of every town and city; and even their Roman Catholic faith and their language — all of which came with the Spanish *conquistadores*. And they rarely mention Cortés, who founded *mestizo* Mexico after conquering the Aztec empire. There are no streets or towns named after him, no statues in his honor. Mexico's Spanishness is everywhere in its culture, but its Indian heritage is what Mexicans stress as being most distinctly Mexican.

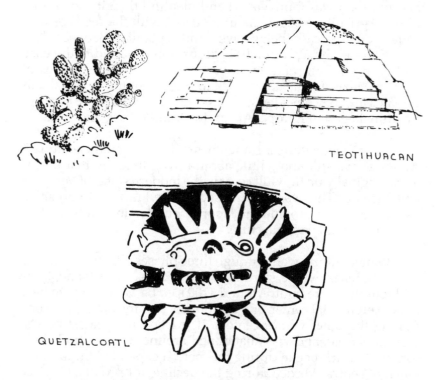

TEOTIHUACAN

QUETZALCOATL

What we know about that Indian heritage is still spotty, but it is constantly and rapidly being revised and expanded as new literary and archeological discoveries are made. Certain aspects of the Aztec Empire were recorded by the Spanish, but not all. The history of pre-Aztec times has been particularly obscure. This is partly because most of its cultures were overthrown and partly because its written history not inscribed in stone was burned, first by the Aztec conqueror Itzcoatl and then with religious fervor by the Spanish. History is always written by the victors, but luckily later Mexican revolutionaries rarely burned books they disagreed with; like most revolutionaries, they just read them selectively.

Although hunter-gatherer tribes probably lived in Mexico from very early in the human habitation of the Americas, the first trace has been found near Mexico City and dates by radiocarbon test to about 21,000 B.C. People settled in the Valley of Mexico because food was more varied and plentiful than it was farther north. Agriculture began about 6000 B.C., with the seeds of wild squash and avocado being saved and replanted. Between 5000 and 3500 B.C. the aboriginal Mexicans domesticated both beans and corn (*maize*); *chiles* were gathered. Thus these staples of today's Mexican cuisine go back to the beginning of social culture in Mexico. Coincidentally, this was about the same time agriculture began in Europe, Africa, the Middle East, and Asia.

The Olmec culture is sometimes called the "mother culture," Although we still know little about it, we do know that it centered originally on the Gulf coast in the modern states of Veracruz and Tabasco. This was the first society we know of to organize itself in order to provide the labor to build community centers with monumental architecture.

Olmec culture went through three phases. The first centered on San Lorenzo, where, starting around 1200 B.C., courts and pyramid temples were built. Around 1100 B.C., La Venta grew to be a larger ceremonial center, and it probably became the capital controlling the other Olmec centers. It reached its greatest power around 900 B.C. and was abandoned around 300 B.C. Trade and conquest which began during this period expanded throughout much of central Mexico during the decline of La Venta. Distinctive artworks of the first two periods were colossal stone heads typically with broad flat noses and thick lips and carvings of jaguar gods and man-jaguar figures. These latter indicate the rise of a jaguar cult which would be important in Mexican culture until the coming of Christianity 2500 years later. During the last pe-

This rough outline of Mexican history may help you hold onto the details in the narrative history in this section.

up to 1500 B.C.	**The Archaic period.** First settlements. Agriculture begins. Corn is discovered.
1500–300 B.C.	**The Pre-Classic period.** The first pottery. Starting around 1200 B.C., the Olmecs develop "the mother culture," the foundation for all later cultures.
300 B.C.–900 A.D.	**The Classic Period.** Three great cultures flourish in different parts of Mexico: The Monte Albán Zapotec in Oaxaca, the Maya in the Yucatán and south, and from 100 to 900 A.D. the Teotihuacan.
900–1520 A.D.	**The Post-Classic Period.** A succession of warlike northern nomadic tribes, generally called Chichimecs, establish cities throughout Mexico: the Toltecs (900–1150), the Mixtecs of Monte Albán (1200–), the Tepanecs (1320–), and finally the Mexicas or Aztecs, who founded their city, Tenochtitlán (Mexico City), in Lake Texcoco and became independent of the Tepanecs in 1376.
1420–1521 A.D.	**The Aztec Empire.**
1519–1521 A.D.	**The Conquest.** Cortés conquers the Aztecs. The colony of New Spain (Mexico) lasts 300 years.
1810–1821 A.D.	**The War of Independence.** Spanish colonial rule is overthrown; a complicated century of dictatorships, republican reforms, and foreign incursions follows.
1910–1920 A.D.	**The Revolution.** Social, economic, and political reform under one-party rule. That party, reorganized as the PRI in 1929, is still in power.

riod of La Venta's decline and Olmec decentralization, Olmec culture developed mural painting, a writing system, astronomical/mathematical calculations which show that they understood the concept of zero, and a calendar. All of these were passed through trade and conquest to the Olmecs' contemporaries and through them to later cultures. The term *mother culture* seems appropriate. In the old world, the Olmec period began about the time of Tutankhamen's death in Egypt in 1323 and lasted until the fall of Persia to Alexander in 332 B.C.

The period following the final collapse of Olmec power is often called the Classical period. It started around 100 B.C. Three great cultures coexisted: The Monte Albán Zapotec in Oaxaca, the Maya in the Yucatan and south, and from 100 to 900 A.D. the Teotihuacan. The least is known of the culture of the Zopotecs, which had its roots as early as 500 B.C. overlapping the Olmecs. There greatest city, Monte Albán, was rich and powerful. Both its art and architecture showed the influence of the late Olmecs and then of the other classical cultures. The earliest literary texts that have been found were written by the Zapotecs, a striking innovation. More insights will surely be discovered in the next few years.

Much effort and money has been devoted to exploring the second great classical culture, the Maya. This is partly because the great Maya ruins have become major tourist attractions. In recent years many different discoveries have revised our understanding of the Maya culture that followed the Olmec. Originally seen as a peaceful society ruled by priest and scholars, the society is now understood to have been dominated by warring city states ruled by bloody warlords.

Beginning around 300 B.C., the Mayas adapted and made their own most of Olmec culture. Their art, their temples, their writing, math, and science, and their political and military skills were all dramatic and vigorous, but it is the innovations they made in agriculture and the population explosion that came with them that were most astounding. We are just beginning to understand their accomplishment. They cleared the jungle and farmed much of what is now the Yucatán, Belize, and Guatamala, providing the wealth and surplus labor needed to build their many city centers. These were made up of stone palaces, pyramid temples, and the sacred ball courts which later became fixtures in most of the urban centers of Mesoamerica. By 600 A.D. it is estimated that the population of this 36,000-square-mile Maya "empire" had a density of 600 people per square mile, similar to the most densely populated areas of rural China today. Shortly after it peaked around 750 A.D., the population collapsed. Two-thirds were gone by 850 A.D., and by 1100 A.D. the region was sparsely populated and the cities were being slowly engulfed by the jungle. There are many theories as to why this happened. Soil exhuastion, drought, and disease probably all played a part. Certainly the constant wars, culminating in the late classical period with the war between the royal families of Tikal and Calakmul around 700 A.D., may have started the decline.

Like the people of many other early civilizations around the world, those of all the early Mexican cultures, starting with the Olmecs, studied the stars. Rituals relating to tracking the stars and predicting celestial events and the seasons were central to their religions and to their understanding of history. The Mayas, whose calendar was in some ways more accurate than our own, were the most sophisticated astronomers of the premodern world. Much later, the giant Aztec calendar stone, now in the Anthropology Museum in Mexico City, shows that the religious importance of these studies continued until the Conquest.

In all of the pre-Hispanic Mexican cultures, the seasons and all other vital natural phenomena were understood to be controlled by or to be attributes of the gods. Huitzilopochtli, one of the most important Aztec gods, was the god to whom human sacrifices were made to keep the sun coming up each day. Another vital force was Tlaloc, the god of rain and thunder.

Not all of the Mexican gods were identified with nature; not all had bloody sacrificial rites. One of the strongest was Quetzalcoatl. He first appears as a great feathered serpent with a huge temple compound at Teotihuacan, a city of temples or, as the Aztecs later called it, "the city of the gods." (Mysteriously, *teo* means "god" in both Indo-European languages and in Nahuatl, the Aztec indigenous language.) Today the temples have been uncovered, but the surrounding city awaits the archeologists.

45

© Tatiana Parcero, 1995. Credit: Mexican Government Tourism Office.

At the heart of Mexico City, which is the heart of Mexico, is the Zócalo. This was the sacred central square of Tenochtitlan, the island capital of the Aztec empire. Cortés tore down much of the great pyramid, the Templo Mayor, with its twin temples to the patron war god, Huitzilopochtli, and Tlaloc, the god of rain. Then, symbolically, he used its stones to build a cathedral on its ruins. The present cathedral, on the left in the photograph above, replaced that of Cortés. Started in 1562, it took 250 years to complete. To its right is its parish church, El Sagrario. Built of dark red stone, called "blood stone" by the Aztecs, it is a masterpiece of the ultrabaroque style. Continuing to the right are the ruins of the Great Temple. The Zócalo is formally known as the Plaza de la Constitución, but it is more commonly known by its old Aztec name, as are the central squares of other towns around Mexico. In the past, the Zócalo has been a formal garden and a parade ground, but now it is paved — a huge traffic circle, full of life but not elegant, considering that it is the center of both the nation's religious and political life. The enormous National Palace is the historic house of government and the office of the President. Although it is built on the site of the palace of Aztec emperor, Moctezuma, tourists now visit to see the great murals of Diego Rivera showing the history of Mexico from its Indian culture through the Conquest to the Revolution.

Tenochtitlan and its twin city Tlatelolco were build safely on islands in the middle of a vast lake, Texcoco. The lake was named after a city on the shore that was first an enemy and then, after a long war, a minor third partner to the capitals. Tenochtitlan was the political/military capital of the Aztec empire, while Tlatelolco was its commercial capital. They were connected to the mainland by bridges that could be raised against enemies and by long aqueducts. The Aztecs ate fish, birds, and insects from the clean waters of the lake. All around their cities they built chinampas, floating gardens fertilized by the waste of the cities, which they kept out the cities' canals. The gardens gave the cities a source of fresh vegetables and flowers year round that was safe from enemies on the shore of the lake — safe because Texcoco was protected by the Aztec naval fleet of war canoes.

Since the Conquest, Texcoco has been polluted, drained, and filled. Flying into Mexico City, you can still see its remains, mud and salt flats now being filled with city sprawl. One part of the old Aztec lake has been preserved, however. It is Xochimilco. There you can take a trajinera or "flower boat" like the one in the photograph below. These gondola-like craft have women's names, like the "Gabriela." They follow winding ways among the ancient floating gardens. Xochimilco is a favorite site for Sunday picnics with its strolling mariachis, floating food stands, and lively crowds of Mexicans and visitors.

© Tatiana Parcero, 1995. Credit: Mexican Government Tourism Office.

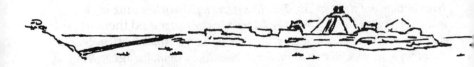

Teotihuacan had about 200,000 people and was not only the largest city of the Americas but, at its peak, the largest in the world. Around 650 a.d., this greatest city of the Classic Period was sacked by northern nomads. Its people scattered, taking their belief in Quetzalcoatl with them.

In about 900 A.D., a nomadic tribe called the Toltecs settled in the Valley of Mexico and adopted Quetzalcoatl, who was not a war god but a bringer of peace and of all the civilized arts. A hundred years later a light-skinned, bearded, blue-eyed man came to the Toltecs, was accepted as their priest-king, and revealed himself as Quetzalcoatl incarnate. He moved his capital to Tula and expanded his empire and his religion throughout central Mexico. Then he was ousted from power after a mythological struggle with his rival Texcatlipoca, the god of war. This man and his followers escaped to Cholula and then built Chichen Itza in Maya country. Finally, he sailed away to the east but promised to return and rule all of Mexico in peace on his birth year in the next calendar cycle, the year "one-reed" or 1519.

With the sack of Tula in about 1150, Toltec power declined, but their city remained a center for the worship of Quetzalcoatl. In 1320 the Tepanecs consolidated control of central Mexico. Then the Mexicas or Aztecs rose to power. They had first ended their nomadic wandering around 1325 when they saw a sign foretold years before, an eagle eating a snake while sitting on a cactus. (This vision, an odd twist on the feathered serpent, is now the symbol of the modern Mexican state.) The Aztecs found their eagle on an island in Lake Texcoco, and there they built their island city, Tenochtitlan (now Mexico City). In 1376 they won independence from the Tepanecs. Then, starting in 1420, they began the bloody conquest of their neighbors. Within 100 years they ruled the largest of all the Mesoamerican empires.

Then came the year "one-reed." Moctezuma, the devout priest-emperor of the Aztecs, nervously awaited the second coming of Quetzalcoatl. As if on cue, Hernan Cortés and his white, bearded men arrived. Moctezuma naturally greeted them as gods and sent gifts of gold, turquoise, and the feathers of the *quetzal* bird, sacred to Quetzalcoatl. With incredible courage, imagination, and greed, Cortés decided to seize the empire and the source of the gold. He had horses and steel swords and guns, all of which the Aztecs lacked. Despite these advantages, Cortés and his small band of soldiers would never have been able to defeat Moctezuma's vast army without the additional manpower of their Indian allies, subject cities that rebelled against the severe rule of the Aztec central government. The history of the fall of the Aztec Empire is so dramatic it reads like fiction. Once the Aztec government was destroyed, Cortés swiftly and skillfully substituted a Spanish, Christian empire for the Aztec one. It lasted for three hundred years.

It is said that the Mexico of today was formed during this colonial period of the country's history. Many cities and towns were founded; universities were begun; and Spanish crafts, art, and architecture were everywhere. The Roman Catholic Church and its Inquisition converted the Indians integrating the native symbols and beliefs into Mexican Christianity. On the great central plateau, the Spaniards and various Indian races began the long process of amalgamation which is still going on today.

After Cortés, New Spain, as it was called, was ruled by a series of viceroys who had absolute power. Their form of government still influences Mexico today in that its presidents wield tremendous power (by U.S. standards). The land was divided up between various Spanish supporters of the viceroys, and those who were granted the land also had power over the Indians who were living there. Second only to the crown in power was the Church, which by 1821 owned 50% of the property and capital of the country.

There were no serious movements to overthrow Spanish rule in Mexico until Napoleon's army invaded Spain in 1808 and the legitimate Spanish monarchy collapsed. On September 15, 1808,

Father Miguel Hidalgo called his people together and raised the banner of the Virgin of Guadalupe with the cry: "*¡Mexicanos, viva México!*" This action started off a rebellion that was to end on September 9, 1821, with *La Independencia,* the country's independence from Spain. Agustín de Iturbide was then elected regent. A few months later, he dissolved the congress and proclaimed himself Emperor of Mexico, taking the title of "Agustín I." He was quickly exiled. Then, like Napoleon, he returned in the hope of reclaiming his throne. This time he was tried and shot.

After Mexico had existed as a constitutional republic for nearly ten years after the death of Iturbide, General Antonio López de Santa Ana organized a revolt, abolished the federalist constitution, and set up a centralized government. It was during this time of Santa Ana that Texas was separated from the Mexican state of Coahuila. Soon more and more "*gringos*" moved into Texas, leading eventually to a war between Mexico and the U.S. in 1836. At first Santa Ana was successful in his war — he took the Alamo from the U.S. Texans — but then he was captured at San Jacinto and sold back to his country. Texas declared itself to be independent. Later, in 1845, the U.S. annexed Texas and then provoked Mexico to attack this new U.S. territory. In response, the U.S. declared war, invaded Mexico itself, and captured Mexico City. Early in 1848, the war ended, with Mexico losing not only Texas but also the land that now constitutes California, Arizona, New Mexico, and Nevada — in all, about half of its territory. This action, one year before the 1849 Gold Rush, is still deeply resented

During the many years of anarchy and civil war that followed, one of Mexico's greatest heroes emerged — Benito Juárez, who would become one of Mexico's most significant presidents. A man of Indian origin and humble beginnings, Juárez rose through the Justice Department to become president during one of Mexico's most difficult periods. After the fall of Santa Ana, he tried to unify Mexico under the Constitution of 1857. When he refused to recognize the rebel leaders of the Conservative Party who opposed the constitution, Juárez was forced to flee to Panama. However, he returned to Veracruz and passed the Re-

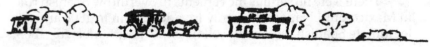

© 1995 by Tatiana Parcero. Credit: Mexican Government Tourism Office.

The Paseo de la Reforma is the most formal, most official street in Mexico City. Lined with flower beds and palm trees, embassies and fine hotels, it moves from one monumental circle to another across the center of the city until it ends at spacious Chapultepec Park with its Castle and museums — the Museo Nacional de Anthropologia is one of the wonders of the world and not to be missed. In each of the circles of the Reforma there is a monument. A statue of Cuauhtémoc, the last Aztec emperor, overlooks the circle where Reforma crosses another major road, Insurgentes. The most famous monument, a symbol of Mexico City, is the Monumento de la Independencia, known familiarly as "El Angel." A 150-foot pillar topped with an angel is surrounded by statues of the leading figures who won Mexico's independence from Spain.

form Laws separating church and state. This policy plunged Mexico into a three-year civil war that eventually bankrupted the country. Mexico was forced to suspend payments on loans from Spain, France, and England.

In response, Spanish, French, and British military forces entered Mexico in 1862 to negotiate their debts. After the Spanish and British had left, the French stayed on and began an invasion of the country. In 1863, the French placed the Austrian Archduke Maximilian in power and declared Mexico a monarchy. However, Maximilian was able to hold onto power only as long as the French troops supported him. As the U.S. Civil War ended, Juárez asked the U.S. to enforce the Monroe Doctrine and demand a French withdrawal. Lincoln did. With difficulties in France and the implied threat of the huge, successful U.S. army to the north, Napoleon III removed his troops from Mexico, leaving Maximilian with only a small contingent of conservative forces. In 1867, Juárez' army defeated Maximilian at Queretaro and executed him. In 1872, Benito Juárez died in office, leaving an unstable government. However, Juárez had a profound and lasting effect on Mexico through his struggle to build an independent and just democracy. He is considered to be Mexico's Abraham Lincoln.

In 1876, Porfirio Díaz assumed the Mexican presidency, and he remained as head of state either directly or through a puppet president for the following 30 years. His efficient military and his strong, centralized rule made Mexico safe for the wealthy and foreign travelers, but he tolerated no political opposition. Pressures for liberalization and democratic change were repressed, as they were in the U.S. and Europe during the same period. Revolutions were kept down by brutally crushing peasants' rights. The common people of Mexico, whom Juárez had championed, were perhaps worse off than ever. Land and power were still in the hands of a few, while many peasants led miserable lives of hunger and destitution.

At the same time, the Díaz government forced modernization on Mexico. It encouraged new technology and industry, which it financed by foreign investment and trade. It was during this time that most of Mexico's railroads were built. For the first time in history, the country had a balanced budget. Mexico appeared on the outside to be peaceful and prosperous, and this was widely accepted as a blessing after several generations of civil war and stagnation. However, the political and social price was too high; the country was sitting on a powder keg ready to explode. Of course, Mexico was not alone in this. At this same time, revolution was a real possibility in most European countries, and Russia and China were ready to blow. When Francisco Madero won the election of 1910, Díaz tried to wrest power from him by force, but Madero kept the presidency and Don Porfirio fled to Europe.

Many warring factions were struggling for power in 1910. Again Mexico faced civil war. For ten terrible years, there was anarchy and assassination. The presidency was passed from one man to another. Pancho Villa and Emiliano Zapata led revolts in the north and south. Their peasant armies looted and burned the rich haciendas where at one time they had worked. Much property was destroyed in the name of the Revolution. The poor of the cities and countryside suffered as much as the rich and middle class. Much of the economy was destroyed. Finally, with the nation exhausted, elections were held, and General Alvaro Obregón was elected president in 1920. He restored peace and began to build rural schools and increase industrial and agricultural production.

In 1929, the **Partido Revolucionario Institucional** (PRI) was founded under the Portes Gil administration. This political party successfully took over control of the central govenment from the military and provided Mexico with a strong political institution. Since the founding of the PRI, only civilians have been elected to office, and there have been no military revolts. Although there are opposition parties with local and regional power bases, the PRI has maintained one-party control of the central government under an extremely powerful presidency. They have discouraged any strong opposition and until recently were still in complete

control.

In 1934, during the worldwide economic depression, Lázaro Cárdenas was elected president. Cárdenas increased school construction and land distribution among peasants. In 1938, he nationalized the petroleum industry by ousting American and British oil companies. He improved labor conditions and met the demands of workers, which had long been neglected.

Although there have been some regional outbreaks of rebellion and lawlessness, Mexico has generally been at peace since 1920, enjoying stable governments and making advancements in industry and agriculture. In recent years, however, corruption from the central government on down to local officials has shaken the faith of many of the people. At the same time, Mexico faces many serious social, political, and economic challenges. Recent social and political turmoil in Chiapas and the dramatic bailout of the Mexican ecomony by the International Monetary Fund (IMF) are examples. After nearly 70 years, the grip of the PRI, caught in a series of scandals and economic crises, seems to be weakening. In July 1997, for the first time, the PRI lost control the lower house of Congress, the Chamber of Deputies, and of the government of Mexico City. Cuauhtémoc Cárdenas, Lazaro's son, became mayor, giving him and his center-leftist DRP (Democratic Revolutionary Party) the second most powerful political position in Mexico. In response, the PRI is making some economic, fiscal, and political reforms in an attempt to become more democratic and less corrupt and to hold onto the presidency.

The problems facing Mexico are very serious. The population growth of Mexico City, with its dangerous air and water polution, is out of control. With 24 million inhabitants, it is the largest single city in the world. There is social and political unrest in many parts of the country. Still, at present there is hope. The Mexican people are making real progress in increasing trade and economic stability; under the political and financial struggles of the moment, there is a strong and unified national feeling. And Mexicans look to their colorful history for inspiration and a source of pride.

3.2 Map: Cities of Mexico

3.3 People

Mexico is the most populous Spanish-speaking country in the world with a population of about 100 million. It is the second most populous country in Latin America (after Brazil). More than one half of the people live in central Mexico. Three quarters of the population lives in cities while the rest live in rural areas. About 65 percent of the people are a mixture of Indian and Spanish, making Mexico one of the most *mestizo* countries in Latin America. About a quarter of the population is Indian.

Many Mexicans emigrate from areas lacking in job opportunities, such as in the underdeveloped southern states and the crowded central plateau, and go to the industrialized urban centers and the developing border areas of the northern states.

According to estimates, the urban population of Mexico City has grown to more than 24 million, making it the largest urban concentration in the world. Guadalajara is the second largest city with about 6 million people. Monterrey and other urban areas in the northern region of the country also show large increases in population.

Many cities and towns resemble those of Spain. The *plaza* or main square of most towns is planned in the same fashion, with a garden, complete with a bandstand and park benches, surrounded by a church (sometimes a cathedral), public buildings, and restaurants. The plaza is a convenient public place where people congregate to socialize and on special occasions. Traditionally, the Sunday *paseo* around the plaza was a social event where the unmarried young people came to see and be seen.

3.4 Land and Climate

Mexico has varied climates, including tropical, temperate, and some colder areas. The topography of Mexico ranges from low desert plains and jungle-like coastal strips to high plateaus and rugged mountains. Beginning at the Isthmus of Tehuantepec in southern Mexico, an extension of a South American mountain range runs north almost to Mexico City, where it divides to form the coastal *Occidental* (west) and *Oriental* (east) ranges of the Sierra Madre. Between these ranges lies the great central plateau, the Valley of Mexico, a rugged tableland 2400 kilometers (1500 miles) long and as much as 800 kilometers (500 miles) wide. From a low desert plain in the north, it rises to 2400 meters (8000 feet) above sea level near Mexico City.

Historic Sites   1. Teotihuacan   2. El Tajín   3. Monte Albán
4. Palenque   5. Uxmal   6. Chichén Itzá   7. Coba   8. Tulum

Geographical Features   9. Popocatépetl   10. Citlatépetl
11. Sierra Madre Occidental   12. Sierra Madre Oriental
13. Sierra Madre del Sur

Mexico's climate is generally more closely related to altitude and rainfall than to latitude. Most of Mexico is dry; only about 12% of the total area receives adequate rainfall in all seasons, while about one-half is deficient in moisture throughout the year. Temperatures range from 60° to 100°F (15.5° to 37.7°C) in tropical areas, whereas the weather in the higher elevations may be damp and cold. Many areas of central Mexico experience a dry season during the winter months and a rainy season in the summer. Pack accordingly. You will want warm-weather clothing, a water-repellent topcoat, and perhaps a warm sweater that you can put on or peel off as the weather and comfort dictate. Footwear for both dress and rugged terrain (including cobblestoned streets) are important.

3.5 Government

Mexico consists of 31 states and a federal district. It is officially called *Estados Unidos Mexicanos* ("the United Mexican States") and is often referred to as *"la República de México"* ("the Republic of Mexico").

Mexico's federal government has three branches: the legislative, executive, and j udicial. The legislative branch consists of a General Congress made up of two chambers, the Senate and the Chamber of Deputies. There are two senators for each state and two for the Federal District. Neither senators nor deputies may be re-elected for a succeeding term. The constitution provides that the Congress legislate on all matters pertaining to the national government, the territories, and the Federal District.

The president is elected by popular vote for a period of six years and may not be re-elected. The president of Mexico wields much more power than the president does in the United States. In Mexico, he makes all important decisions and is the principal lawmaker in the nation. He can declare war and decree new laws. Like the U.S. president, he also upholds the laws of Congress, appoints high government officials, commands the military, and conducts foreign affairs. There are 16 executive departments: Attorney General, Interior, State, National Defense, Navy, Treasury,

National Patrimony, Commerce and Industry, Agriculture, Communications, Public Works, Hydraulic Resources, Education, Public Health, Labor, and the Secretariat of the Presidency.

The Judiciary consists of a Supreme Court, the highest court in the country, and district and circuit courts.

There are many political parties in Mexico, but only the *Partido Revolucionario Institucional* (**PRI**), has held the presidency. Until 1997, the PRI also had complete control of the Congress. It has been the most important political force in the nation for nearly 70 years.

3.6 Economy

The Mexican economy is still firmly based on agriculture even though industry has advanced greatly in recent years. The government controls most of the larger farms and has funded huge irrigation projects. Ma jor crops are corn, coffee, sugar, and cotton. Petroleum is one of Mexico's most valuable natural resources and its major export Others are coffee and winter vegetables. Mexico was the first Latin American country to become an important oil producer. Mexican industry now includes petrochemicals and pharmaceuticals, as well as steel, trucks, automobiles, textiles, and appliances.

In the 1980s, the collapse of world oil prices caused severe problems for the Mexican economy. During the 1970s, the government had extended social benefits and other government spending, along with monumental graft and corruption. With the expected oil income lost, the national debt suddenly ballooned to huge proportions. However, the international manufacturing sites in the north have continued to boom, and the signing of the North American Free Trade Agreement (NAFTA) between Mexico, Canada, and the United States, on January 1, 1994, has curtailed inflation, which dropped from 114.2% in 1988 to around 7% in December 1994. This trade liberalization agreement brought new vigor to the economy and helped broaden the tax base. Working closely with the World Bank and the international banking commmunity, the government has become fiscally more conservative and has reduced the national debt. Starting in 1998, however, this stability has been threatened by economic instability in Asia, Eastern Europe, and South America.

Despite the economic recovery, Mexicans remain nervous about the *peso*, particularly because of continuing fears of political instability in the country. There are other reasons for this anxiety, too. Before it was brought down, inflation had wiped out many people's savings. For most Mexicans, the standard of living is lower than it was in the 1970s. The population explosion in Mexico — particularly among the poor, where large families are still the rule—has also contributed to economic, social, and political instability over the last quarter of a century.

3.7 Education

About 1,500 years ago, the Mayans correctly measured and registered the weather so that they could predict the seasons using a calendar developed by observing the stars. They also developed the Olmec system for mathematics into one of remarkable sophistication. With such a background, it is hard to believe that Mexicans did not do much about public education until the twentieth century. This failure was due in part to the long dominance of foreign powers. Certainly the Spaniards were not keen on educating the Indians (with the exception of the children of the heads of government). They feared that if the Indians learned too much, Spanish colonial control would be more difficult to maintain. Therefore, the Indians were primarily taught about religion. However, there has always been a core of Mexican culture that has valued learning. As early as 1551, the Viceroy Luís de Velasco prepared the statutes necessary for the establishment of the National University of Mexico and also established the first printing press in the New World.

Benito Juárez, the Zapotec Indian who became President of Mexico, implemented several changes, including a program of free public education in 1860. This program still exists today. Implementing public education has not always been easy or politically popular, and both Church and State struggled to delineate educational responsibilities. In 1944, Manuel Avila Camacho, the president, started a national campaign requiring every Mexican between 18 and 60 years of age who knew how to read and write to teach another Mexican (6 to 60 years old). Camacho made free books available to everyone. Children taught their parents, secretaries taught porters, and housewives taught their maids. The program was established to last for one year, but the campaign continued much longer. As a result, the index of illiteracy diminished by 75%.

Education in Mexico is being decentralized and expanded. A major attempt is under way to promote educational activity in rural areas, and the increase in school enrollments since 1970 has been dramatic. In 1980, 86% of the population between ages 6 and 14 were in school — 16 million children.

Mexicans are proud of their schools and the progress of their educational system. Public education is free, including agricultural and vocational schools. There are also numerous universities, which are well attended. Public schooling consists of five years of elementary school, five of secondary, and two of preparatory, prior to entering the university. The first ten years of schooling are mandatory, but they are not always available to the poor in remote areas or in the slums of the great cities.

3.8 Religion

Mexican law provides for freedom of religion. However, almost 90% of Mexicans are Roman Catholic, including many Indian tribes which combine their old customs with Christian beliefs. Paradoxically, some Mexicans also resent the Church because until the twentieth century it was very powerful and very conservative, resisting all kinds of reform. The Revolution and the government since then have had an "anticlerical" bias and have tried to keep the Church out of politics. In general, Mexicans feel both a resistance and a strong devotion to the Church.

Credit: Mexican Government Tourism Office.

In Guadalajara, Mexico's second largest city, there are many beautiful churches like this one. The Cathedral is the center of the city, surrounded on all four sides by parks and gardens. Started in 1618, it was built in a wonderful mixture of architectural styles and with splendid silver and gold decoration appropriate to the fabulous wealth of New Spain, as Mexico was then called. Nearby are the Iglesia de San Augustin and the Iglesia de Nuestra Señora de Aranazazú on the Parque San Francisco.

Mexico has some of the most beautiful churches in the world. The cathedral of Mexico City, the first in Mexico, is more than 450 years old having been started in 1525. Several sections have been added and today it is the largest church in the country. *La Virgen de Guadalupe* (the Virgin of Guadalupe) is the Patron Saint of Mexico and of the Americas, and a basilica was built in her honor. In 1531 the Virgin appeared to Juan Diego, an Indian, atop a small hill to the north of the city. The Virgin told Juan Diego that she wanted a church built at that spot, and Juan took this message to the bishop. It took several other apparitions before the bishop believed the story. The Virgin finally appeared painted on Juan's blanket, showing Indian features unlike the traditional European images of virgins. Today, many people visit the the old Basilica started in 1536 and the huge, ultramodern New Basilica built in 1976 to house the miraculous painting of the Virgin. There are many sightseers, but most Mexicans come to pray and to seek favors of the Virgin.

Besides Christmas, which continues for twelve days ending with Epiphany (Day of the Wise Kings), and Holy Week (Palm Sunday through Easter), Mexico celebrates many other religious holidays. There is even a day for the animals (San Roque) when people take their animals to be blessed by the priests. In general, people are quite observant of religious customs in Mexico, and religion is an important part of their daily lives.

3.9 Arts

Mexican art is among the most diverse and beautiful in the world. Its different manifestations — whether in architecture, painting, sculpture, weaving, or other forms — reveal great influence from their Spanish heritage and even more from their Mayan, Aztec, and other Indian origins. Each region of the country has produced its own specific types of folk art, open displayed in museums all over the world. The tradition of Mexican folk art is one of the richest in the Americas. Handicrafts are taught in schools, and every school child knows something about folk art and crabs. Twentieth-century Mexican art is probably best known for the works of its many famous muralists, such as David Alfaro Siquieros, Diego Rivera, Rufino Tamayo, and Clemente Orozco.

Mexican artists and intellectuals alike have consistently drawn inspiration from a rich history of Indian civilizations, colonial influence, revolution, and the development of the modern Mexican state. In turn, Mexican art has influenced every aspect of Mexican life. Its influences in modern design (clothing and interior decorating) are very marked, as is its artistic influence in public displays, architecture, and the like.

Mexican art can be seen in churches, museums, art galleries, and public buildings all over Mexico. However, the greatest concentration is in Mexico City. The National Art Museum and the *Museo Franz Mayer* have wide-ranging collections. Murals can be seen at the *Museo Mural Diego Rivera*, at the National Palace (offices of the president and government) on the *Zócalo* or central plaza of the city, and at the *Palacio de Bellas Artes*, where the wonderful *Ballet Folklórico de Mexico* performs. Also at the *Zócalo* are the *Catedral Metropolitana* and the *Sagrario Church.* Around the corner, for everyone interested in ancient Mexico, are the ruins of the Great Temple of the Aztecs, *el Templo Mayor,* and its new museum.

Finally, no trip to Mexico City is complete without a visit to the National Musuem of Anthropology in Chapultepec Park, without argument one of the very finest museums in the world.

4. The Spanish Language

Spanish belongs to the Romance family of languages — along with French, Italian, Portuguese, and several others. These languages all have their origins in ancient Latin. Other languages, like Greek, Italian, French, and Arabic, have also exerted some influence on Spanish. With the discovery of the New World, Spanish was brought to the Americas, where, over the centuries, it borrowed many words from its contact with the indigenous tongues. In recent years, Spanish has also borrowed from English, as well as contributing many words to the English language. It is no wonder that many Spanish words may seem familiar to you.

Nearly 3 billion people speak Spanish, the world's fourth major language. Spanish is spoken over a vast area from Spain to the Americas, including Mexico, Central America, the Caribbean, South America (except Brazil), and many parts of the United States.

Despite some variation in pronunciation, vocabulary, and grammar, Spanish speakers from different regions can usually understand each other. In addition, in several predominantly Spanish-speaking areas, other languages are sometimes spoken. For example, in Spain — an area about four times that of New York State — Basque (*vasco*), Galician (*gallego*), and Catalan (*catalán*) are spoken, and in Mexico and other Latin American nations, hundreds of indigenous tongues survive.

Spanish spread rapidly throughout the Iberian peninsula in the latter part of the fifteenth century when Fernando de Aragón and Isabel de Castilla married, uniting Spain. Fernando accepted the speech of Castile, making Castilian (or Spanish) the official language of the country. At the same time, the defeat of the Moors in Granada in 1492 diminished Arab influence, which had affected the Spanish tongue for over 700 years. Columbus' historic voyage that same year took Castilian to the New World, and that explains its widespread use today.

In the New World, the language of the *conquistadores* underwent various changes, hastened by its contact with the native

tongues. Many new words for the things unknown to the Peninsular speakers were borrowed, reflecting their "American" experience. In areas of heaviest Indian influence, such as Mexico, Guatemala, and the Andean regions, the new words made Spanish a marvelously expressive and colorful language, which often distinguishes Latin American speech even today. Immigrants from other areas of Europe and the slaves brought from Africa further changed Latin American Spanish. More recently, English has had a profound effect as contact between neighbors north and south increases.

Despite pronunciation and vocabulary variations throughout the Hispanic world, Spanish generally follows the same grammatical patterns everywhere. The Academy of the Spanish Language (*Academia de la Lengua Española*) also strives to maintain consistent standards. Several dialect areas are commonly recognized: central and northern Spain (which use Castilian), southern Spain (whose speech is closer to that of their Caribbean counterparts), Mexico, and the coastal and mountainous regions of Central and South America. Fortunately, regional differences do not normally interfere with communication. When traveling, however, you would do well to follow the patterns of the region you visit.

4.1. A Pronunciation Guide

The chart that follows will be your guide to the transcriptions that follow in this book. Review the chart to see how Spanish sounds are properly pronounced.

Three points should be emphasized about the chart.

1. Fortunately, the Spanish spelling system is much more phonetic than English. Its rules are simple and consistent.
2. Pay special attention to vowels, since they affect the overall pronunciation of a word and are crucial to making yourself understood. Vowels are generally shorter and crisper in Spanish.
3. Note that word stress is indicated by showing the syllable to be accentuated in capital letters, as in this example: *turista* (too-REES-tah).

Vowels

Spanish spelling	Approximate sound in English	Symbol	Transcription example
a	(f<u>a</u>ther)	ah	*turista* (too-REES-t<u>ah</u>)
e	(s<u>ay</u>)	ay	*peso* (P<u>AY</u>-soh)
e	(m<u>e</u>t)	eh	*cerca* (S<u>EH</u>R-kah)
i	(b<u>ee</u>t)	ee	*día* (D<u>EE</u>-ah)
o	(b<u>o</u>th)	oh	*foto* (F<u>OH</u>-toh)
u	(b<u>oo</u>th)	oo	*mucho* (M<u>OO</u>-choh)

Frequent Vowel Combinations (Diphthongs)

ai	(t<u>i</u>pe)	y	*bailar* (by-LAHR)
au	(n<u>ow</u>)	ow	*auto* (<u>OW</u>-toh)
ei	(m<u>ay</u>)	ay	*peine* (P<u>AY</u>-nay)
ie	(<u>y</u>et)	yeh	*siempre* (S<u>YEH</u>M-pray)
oy	(s<u>oy</u> sauce)	oy	*estoy* (ehs-T<u>OY</u>)
ue	(<u>we</u>t)	weh	*bueno* (B<u>WEH</u>-noh)

Consonants

b/d/k/l/m/n/p/s/t	similar to English	
c* (before *e/i/y*)	soft *s* sound (s̲ave)	*cine* (s̲EE-nay)
c* (before *a/o/u*)	hard *k* sound (k̲ey)	*cosa* (k̲OH-sah)
cc	*ks* sound (ac̲c̲ept)	*lección* (lehk̲-s̲YON)
ch	hard *ch* sound (c̲h̲amp)	*mucho* (MOO-c̲h̲oh)
g (before *a/o/u*)	hard *g* (g̲o)	*goma* (g̲OH-mah)
g (before *e/i*)	breathy *h* (h̲eat)	*general* (h̲eh-neh-RAHL)
h	always silent	*hasta* (_AHS-tah)
j	breathy *h* (h̲ot)	*José* (h̲oh-SAY)
ll	sound of English *y* (y̲es)	*silla* (see-y̲AH)
ñ	slurred *ny* (can̲y̲on)	*señor* (sehn̲-y̲OR)
qu	as in English *k* (k̲ite)	*que* (k̲ay)
r	single trill	*pero* (PEH-r̲oh)
rr	several trills	*rosa* (r̲r̲OH-sah)
		perro (PEH-r̲r̲oh)
v	as in English *b* (b̲ite)	*vaca* (b̲AH-kah)
x	as in English *ks* (roc̲k̲s)	*taxi* (TAHk̲-s̲ee)
z*	English *s*	*zona* (s̲OH-nah)

*Note: In parts of Spain, *z,* and also *c* before *e/i,* are pronounced like the English *th* (as in t̲h̲ink). Examples: z̲ona (t̲h̲OH-nah), c̲era (t̲h̲EH-rah), c̲inco (t̲h̲EEN-koh). In this book, however, Latin American pronunciation is used throughout, as described in the above chart.

4.2 Some Basic Grammar

Following is a brief outline of the essential features of Spanish.

Articles

Nouns in Spanish are either masculine or feminine. Articles agree in gender and number with the noun.

1. Definite article (the): *el, la, los, las*

	SINGULAR		PLURAL	
MASCULINE	*el niño*	the boy	*los niños*	the boys
FEMININE	*la casa*	the house	*las casas*	the houses

2. Indefinite article (a / an): *un, una, unos, unas*

	SINGULAR		PLURAL	
MASCULINE	*un viaje*	a trip	*unos viajes*	(some) trips
FEMININE	*una carta*	a letter	*unas cartas*	(some) letters

Nouns

1. Most nouns ending in *-o* are masculine. Those ending in *-a* are usually feminine.

   hermano   brother   *hermana*   sister

2. Nouns ending in a vowel add *s* to form the plural; nouns ending in a consonant add **-es**.

   Señora > *Señoras*   *Señor* > *Señores*

3. To show possession, use the preposition *de* (of):

las casas de los señores	the men's houses
la camisa del* niño	the boy's shirt
los zapatos de la niña	the girl's shoes
los zapatos de las niñas	the girls' shoes
la maleta de Juan	John's suitcase

*Note that *del* is the contraction of *de* + *el*.

4. A group including masculine and feminine individuals or items is grammatically masculine:

Un niño y dos niñas son tres niños.
One boy and two girls are three children.

Adjectives

1. Adjectives agree with the nouns they describe in gender and number. Most adjectives form their plurals as do the nouns, by adding -*s* to a vowel ending (usually -*a* or -*o*) and -*es* to a consonant ending.

una casa pequeña	a little (small) house
dos casas pequeñas	two little houses
un niño pequeño	a little boy
dos niños pequeños	two little boys
un libro español	a Spanish book
dos libros españoles	two Spanish books

2. As a rule, the adjective follows the noun.

3. Possessive adjectives

	SINGULAR	PLURAL
my	*mi*	*mis*
your	*tu*	*tus*
his/her/its	*su*	*sus*
our	*nuestro(a)*	*nuestros(as)*
your	*su*	*sus*
their	*su*	*sus*

Possessive adjectives agree with the thing possessed, not with the possessor.

su libro	**his** or **her** or **their** book
su habitación	**his** or **her** or **their** room
sus casas	**his** or **her** or **their** houses

4. Comparative and superlative are formed by adding *más* (*more*) or *menos* (*less*) and *lo más* (*the most*) and *lo menos* (*the least*), respectively, before the adjective.

bonito	beautiful
más bonito	more beautiful
lo más bonito	the most beautiful
menos bonito	less beautiful
lo menos bonito	the least beautiful

Adverbs

These are formed by adding *-mente* to the feminine form of the adjective (if it differs from the masculine); otherwise to the masculine.

lento(a)	slow	*fácil*	easy
lentamente	slowly	*fácilmente*	easily

Adjectives are sometimes used as adverbs, e.g., *fuerte* can mean *strong* or *strongly*.

Pronouns

1. Possessive pronouns:

	SINGULAR	PLURAL
mine	*mío(a)*	*míos(as)*
yours (fam. sing.)	*tuyo(a)*	*tuyos(as)*
yours (polite form)	*suyo(a)*	*suyos(as)*
his/hers/its	*suyo(a)*	*suyos(as)*
ours	*nuestro(a)*	*nuestros(as)*
yours (fam. pl.)	*suyo(a)*	*suyos(as)*
theirs	*suyo(a)*	*suyos(as)*

Possessive pronouns agree with the thing possessed, not with the possessor.

> *María, el libro es tuyo.*   Maria, the book is yours.

2. Demonstrative pronouns:

	MASCULINE	FEMININE	NEUTER
this	*éste*	*ésta*	*esto*
these	*éstos*	*éstas*	*estos*
that	*ése*	*ésa*	*eso*
	aquél	*aquélla*	*aquello*
those	*ésos*	*ésas*	*esos*
	aquéllos	*aquéllas*	*aquellos*

> *Me gusta esto.*   I like this.
> *¡Éstas son casas pequeñas!*   These are little houses!

The above forms are also used as demonstrative adjectives, but written accent marks are dropped from the feminine and masculine forms.

> *Esas niñas van a clase.*   Those girls are going to class.

Mayan pot ritually broken

3. Personal pronouns:

	SUBJECT	DIRECT OBJECT	INDIRECT OBJECT
I	*yo*	*me*	*me*
you (fam.)	*tú*	*te*	*te*
you (polite)	*usted*	*lo*	*se*
he	*él*	*lo*	*le*
she	*ella*	*la*	*le*
it	*él/ella*	*lo/la*	*le*
we	*nosotros(as)*	*nos*	*nos*
you	*ustedes*	*los*	*se*
they	*ellos(as)*	*los*	*les*

Subject pronouns may be omitted, except in the polite forms (***usted, ustedes***) of *you*. ***Tú*** (singular) and *ustedes* (plural) are used when talking to close friends, relatives, children, and among young people; ***usted*** and the same plural, ***ustedes*** (often abbreviated to ***Ud./Uds.***) are used in most other cases.

Verbs

1. Spanish uses two important *auxiliary verbs.* Whereas *ser* can also be used alone, *haber* can only be used with another verb.

ser (to be)*
yo soy (I am)
tú eres (you are)
usted es (you are)
él/ella es (he / she is)
nosotros(as) somos (we are)
ustedes son (you are)
ellos/ellas son (they are)

haber (to have)
yo he (I have)
tú has (you have)
usted ha (you have)
él/ella ha (he / she has)
nosotros(as) hemos (we have)
ustedes han (you have)
ellos/ellas han (they have)

*Note: Spanish has two verbs for *to be*. *Ser* is used to describe a permanent condition. ***Estar*** is used to describe location or a temporary condition.

Mayan pot with jaguar spots

2. **Regular verbs:** There are three main categories of regular verbs:

INFINITIVE:	ends in -ar	ends in -er	ends in -ir
	hablar (to speak)	**comer** (to eat)	**partir** (to leave)
yo	hablo	como	parto
tú	hablas	comes	partes
usted	habla	come	parte
él/ella	habla	come	parte
nosotros	hablamos	comemos	partimos
ustedes	hablan	comen	parten
ellos/ellas	hablan	comen	parten

3. **Irregular verbs:** As in many languages, exceptions have to be learned separately. The following are four common irregular verbs:

INFINITIVE:	**poder** (to be able, can)	**ir** (to go)	**ver** (to see)	**conocer** (to know [a person])
yo	puedo	voy	veo	conozco
tú	puedes	vas	ves	conoces
usted	puede	va	ve	conoce
él/ella	puede	va	ve	conoce
nosotros	podemos	vamos	vemos	conocemos
ustedes	pueden	van	ven	conocen
ellos/ellas	pueden	van	ven	conocen

Negatives

Form the negative by placing no before the verb:
Es difícil.   It's difficult.
No es difícil.   It's not difficult.

Questions

Form questions by changing the intonation of your voice. The personal pronoun is often left out, both in affirmative sentences and in questions:

Hablo español.   I speak Spanish.
¿Hablas español? Do you speak Spanish?

Note: Spanish uses a double question mark. The same is true of exclamation marks:

¡Qué barato!   How cheap!

Question words

Who?	¿Quién?	(kyehn?)
Who? (plural)	¿Quiénes?	(KYEHN-nays?
What?	¿Qué?	(kay?)
Why?	¿Por qué?	(pohr KAY?)
When?	¿Cuándo?	(KWAHN-doh?)
Where?	¿Dónde?	(DOHN-day?)
Where from?	¿De dónde?	(day DOHN-day?)
Where to?	¿Adónde?	(ah-DOHN-day?)
How?	¿Cómo?	(KOH-moh?)
How much?	¿Cuánto?	(KWAHN-toh?)

Who is speaking?   ¿Quién habla?
Where are you going?   ¿Adónde vas?
What's happening? (How's it going?)   ¿Qué pasa?

May/Can ...?

May I have ...?   ¿Puede darme ...?
  or Can you give me ...?
May we have ...?   ¿Puede darnos ...?
Can you show me ...?   ¿Puede enseñarme ...?
Can you tell me...?   ¿Puede decirme ...?
Can you help me, please?   ¿Puede ayudarme, por favor?

Wanting

I'd like ...	Quisiera ...
We'd like ...	Quisiéramos ...
Please give me ...	Por favor, déme ...
Please bring me ...	Por favor, tráigame ...
I'm hungry.	Tengo hambre.
I'm thirsty.	Tengo sed.
I'm tired.	Estoy cansado(a)
I'm lost.	Estoy perdido(a)
It's important.	Es importante.
It's urgent.	Es urgente.
Hurry up!	¡Dése prisa!

It is/There is ...

It is ...	Es ...
Is it ...?	¿Es ...?
It isn't ...	No es ...
There is/There are ...	Hay ...
Is there/Are there ...?	¿Hay ...?
There is no ...	No hay ...
There are no ...	No hay ...

Prepositions and other words

behind	detrás	after	después
to	a	soon	pronto
for	para	already	ya
until	hasta	then	entonces
towards	hacia	again	otra vez
since	desde	there	allí
through	por/a través de	here	aquí
at	a	inside	dentro
in	en/dentro	outside	fuera
with	con	up	arriba
without	sin	above	encima
before	antes	along	a lo largo
between	entre	perhaps	quizá/tal vez
on	sobre/en	not	no

under	*debajo*	nothing	*nada*
none	*ninguno*	nobody	nadie
and	*y*	now	*ahora*
or	*o*	immediately	*inmediatamente*
also	*también*	gladly	*con mucho gusto*

Some common words

cheap / expensive	*barato/caro*
good / bad	*bueno/malo*
better / worse	*mejor/peor*
right / wrong	*correcto/equivocado*
light / heavy	*ligero/pesado*
easy / difficult	*fácil/difícil*
full / empty	*lleno/vacío*
vacant / occupied	*libre/ocupado*
open / shut	*abierto/cerrado*
old / young	*viejo/joven*
old / new	*viejo/nuevo*
big / small	*grande/pequeño*
quick / slow	*rápido/lento*
beautiful / ugly	*bonito/feo*
warm / cold	*caliente/frío*
never / always	*nunca/siempre*
early / late	*temprano/tarde*
near / far	*cerca/lejos*
left / right	*izquierdo/derecho*
yes / no	*sí/no*

Quantities

a little / a lot	*un poco/mucho*
much / many	*mucho/muchos*
more than / less than	*más que/menos que*
enough / too	*bastante/demasiado*
some	*unos/unas*
any	*alguno/alguna*

Numbers

1	*un, uno*	20	*veinte*
2	*dos*	21	*veinte y uno*
3	*tres*	22	*veinte y dos*
4	*cuatro*	30	*treinta*
5	*cinco*	40	*cuarenta*
6	*seis*	50	*cincuenta*
7	*siete*	60	*sesenta*
8	*ocho*	70	*setenta*
9	*nueve*	80	*ochenta*
10	*diez*	90	*noventa*
11	*once*	100	*cien*
12	*doce*	101	*ciento uno*
13	*trece*	110	*ciento diez*
14	*catorce*	200	*doscientos*
15	*quince*	500	*quinientos*
16	*dieciséis*	700	*setecientos*
17	*diecisiete*	900	*novecientos*
18	*dieciocho*	1,000	*mil*
19	*diecinueve*	1,000,000	*un millón*

Time words

What time is it? *¿Que hora es?*

hour	*hora*	year	*año*
day	*día*	yesterday	*ayer*
week	*semana*	today	*hoy*
month	*mes*	tomorrow	*mañana*
Sunday	*domingo*	Thursday	*jueves*
Monday	*lunes*	Friday	*viernes*
Tuesday	*martes*	Saturday	*sábado*
Wednesday	*miércoles*		
January	*enero*	July	*julio*
February	*febrero*	August	*agosto*
March	*marzo*	September	*septiembre*
April	*abril*	October	*octubre*
May	*mayo*	November	*noviembre*
June	*junio*	December	*diciembre*

78

4.3 Some Useful Spanish Expressions

Greetings

Good morning	*Buenos días*	BWEHN-nohs DEE-ahs
Good afternoon	*Buenas tardes*	BWEHN-nahs TAHR-days
Good evening *or* Good night	*Buenas noches*	BWEHN-nahs NOH-chays

Note: In Spanish, *buenas noches* is used both when arriving and when leaving, roughly after 6:00 P.M.

How are you?	*¿Cómo está usted?* KOH-moh ehs-TAH oos-TEHD
My name is ...	*Me llamo ...* MAY YAH-moh ...
What is your name?	*¿Cómo se llama?* KOH-moh say YAH-mah?

Approaching someone

Excuse me,	*Perdone,*	pehr-DOH-nay
• sir	• *señor*	• sehn-YOHR
• ma'am	• *señora*	• sehn-YOH-rah
• miss/ms.	• *señorita*	• sehn-yoh-REE-tah

Do you speak English?	*¿Habla usted inglés?* AH-blah oos-TEHD een-GLAYS?
Do you understand English?	*¿Comprende inglés?* kohm-PREHN-day een-GLAYS?
Yes/No	*Séi/No* see/noh
I'm sorry.	*Lo siento.* loh SYEHN-toh
I don't speak Spanish.	*No hablo español.* noh AH-bloh ehs-pahn-YOHL.
I don't understand.	*No comprendo.* noh kom-PREHN-doh.
I understand a little.	*Comprendo un poco.* kom-PREHN-doh oon POH-koh.

79

I speak very little Spanish.	*Hablo muy poco español.* AH-bloh MOO-ee POH-koh ehs-pahn-YOHL.
Please speak slowly.	*Hable despacio, por favor.* AH-blay dehs-PAH-syoh, pohr fah-BOHR.
Please repeat.	*Repita, por favor.* rray-PEE-tah, pohr fah-BOHR
Thank you.	*Gracias.* GRAH-syahs.

Asking for help

Excuse me.	*Permítame.* pehr-MEE-tah-may.
May I ask a question?	*Una pregunta, por favor.* oo-nah pray-GOON-tah, pohr fah-BOHR
Could you please help me?	*¿Podría ayudarme?* poh-DREE-ah ah-yoo-DAHR-may?

Identifying yourself

I'm a tourist.	*Soy turista.* soy too-REES-tah.
We're tourists.	*Somos turistas.* SOH-mos too-REES-tas.
I'm not from here.	*No soy de aquí.* noh soy day ah-KEE.
I'm from the U.S.	*Soy de los Estados Unidos.* soy day los ehs-TAH-dohs oo-NEE-dohs

I'm from ...	*Soy de ...*	soy day
• New York	• *Nueva York*	• NWAY-bay yohrk
• Philadelphia	• *Filadelfia*	• fee-lah-DEHL-fyah
• Chicago	• *Chicago*	• chee-KAH-goh
• California	• *California*	• kah-lee-FOHR-nya

| I'm North American. | *Soy norteamericano(a).**
soy NOHR-tay-ah-meh-ree-KAHN-oh(ah). |

We're North American.	*Somos norteamericanos(as).* *	SOH-mohs NOHR-tay-ah-meh-ree KAHN-ohs(ahs).

•*Note:* In Spanish, with few exceptions, most nouns and adjectives end in *-o* for male speakers, *-a* for females, with the corresponding plurals *-os* and *-as.* Use *-os* when including both males and females.

Politeness/courtesy

Please	*Por favor.*	pohr fah-BOHR.
Thank you.	*Gracias.*	GRAH-syahs.
You're very kind.	*Muy amable.*	MOO-ee ah-MAH-bleh.
You're welcome.	*De nada.*	day NAH-dah.
Sorry (excuse me).	*Disculpe.*	des-KOOL-pay.
Excuse me.	*Con permiso.*	kohn pehr-MEE-soh.
Good appetite.	*Provecho/Buen provecho.*	proh-BAY-choh / BWEHN proh-BAY-choh.
It doesn't matter.	*No importa.*	Noh ihn-POHR-tah.

Leave-taking

See you soon.	*Hasta pronto.*	AHS-tah PROHN-toh.
So long.	*Hasta luego.*	AHS-tah LWEH-goh.
See you tomorrow.	*Hasta mañana.*	AHS-tah mahn-YAH-nah.
See you later.	*Hasta más tarde.*	AHS-tah mahs TAHR-day.
Good-bye/Bye.	*Adiós.*	ah-DYOHS.

Note: When passing in the street, Mexican friends say, *"Adiós,"* ("Good-bye") instead of "Hello" if they do not intend to stop and speak.

4.4. Gestures

Many gestures are used in Mexico and often not with the same meaning that they have in the United States. For example, to signal someone to come to you, you use a palm-down waving motion of the hand just above waist height. If the hand is a bit higher, it would look similar to North Americans waving goodbye. It is also common to get a waiter's or other attendant's attention with the sound *psst-psst,* a sound that would insult many North Americans.

Mexicans generally don't toss anything when giving it to another person. They always hand things like scissors, pencils, knives, or forks to someone else, with the pointed end toward themselves.

When someone sneezes, Mexicans say "*Salud*" ("Health"). To indicate how tall a person is, they raise their hand with the index finger up, but to show the height of an animal, they hold their hand out with the palm flat and down. Many other gestures are also used to indicate qualities like "crazy," "stingy," "tasty," "nice." Ask someone locally to help you learn these signs.

4.5 Some Typical Mexican Expressions

Mexican Spanish is rich in special expressions and vocabulary, sometimes, unknown in othe rregions where Spanish is spoken. This will give you a start. You may wish to add others to this list:

ahorita/'orita	right away (really means: "in a few moments")
¡ándale!/¡órale!	go ahead; move; you have my permission!
se me antoja	I feel in the mood for … (usually refers to a craving for food)
¡aguas!	watch out! (literally: "Waters!")
botana	snacks; usually at a restaurant, bar, or party
¡qué bronca!	what a mess / problem / pain!
¡qué bruto!	how dumb! also: how amazing! (can be either positive or negative)
me cae bien/mal	I like it/I don't like it
camión	public bus; "*camión de carga*" is for a truck
chamaco(a)	boy / girl
me choca	it disturbs me / it bothers me

un chorro de	a whole lot of … (literally: "a flood of")
chulo(a)	cute
con permiso	excuse me (literally: "with permission")
cuate	friend
escuincle	young kid (sometimes derogatory; from the Nahautl *escuintle*)
fuchi	disgusting / unpleasant
¡qué gacho!	how ugly / how awful!
gringo(a)	a foreigner, often a North American (sometimes derogatory)
güero(a)	blond, fair, or light-skinned (person)
¡híjole!	expression of surprise
¿mande (ud.)?	excuse me, what did you say? (a common and polite expression)
menso(a)	dumb
mordida	a bribe offered in addition to or instead of a fine; "*multa*" is the fine
naco(a)	low-class, ignorant (derogatory)
necio(a)	stupd, dumb
!qué onda!/estar en onda	what a great "ambiance"! to be "with it" Also: what's new? what's going on?
¡qué padre!	great, wonderful!
rajarse	to back out on something, as in "*se rajó*"
tecolote	used to refer to traffic police (literally: "owl")
torta	a sandwich in a roll; "*sanwich*" refers to a sandwich on loaf bread

4.6 A Key to Mexican Menus

Mexican food is great, but tourists sometimes don't try it simply because they don't understand the menu. The following list contains some of the best Mexican appetizers, main dishes, and desserts. Not all of the dishes are spicy, but if you like to avoid spicy dishes, take care to ask the waiter if the item is picante (spicy hot) before ordering. Enjoy!

barbacoa	Although, as the name suggests, this dish is related to barbecue, it is usually mutton with spices, cooked slowly underground in a smothered fire. It is served with *tortillas* and eaten in *tacos.*
burritos	Wheat flour *tortillas* filled with meat or cheese.
cabrito	Kid, young goat, roasted, usually outside, and eaten with *tortillas. Cabrito* is very popular in northern Mexico.
carne asada	Beef, sliced thin and grilled. It is usually served with either corn or wheat *tortillas* and sometimes with *cebollitas* (grilled onion slices). A squeeze of fresh lemon juice is a great addition.
carnitas	Pieces of pork or other meat flavored with spices and cooked slowly until very tender. They are usually served with *tortillas.*
cecina	Dried slices of beef or pork, prepared in all sorts of sauces or grilled.
ceviche	Raw fish or other seafood marinated for hours in lime juice and served in a cocktail with chopped onions, avocado, coriander, cilantro, *chiles,* and tomato.
chicharrón	Fried pork rind. Light and crisp, sometimes salted and spicy, *chicharrónes* are a popular appetizer with *tortillas* and *salsa* (sauce). They are often served with *carnitas* or other cooked meat.
chilaquiles	A popular breakfast dish made of fried *tortilla* chips served in a deep platter covered with a cream sauce. It is always topped with shredded cheese and often with shredded chicken or fried eggs.
chile en nogada	A hot *chile* (pepper) filled with a sweet stuffing, fried, and covered with white cheese, cream sauce, and walnuts. When garnished with pomegranate seeds and fresh parsley, the dish is red, white, and green, representing the Mexican flag.
chile relleno	A hot *chile* (pepper), stuffed with cheese or meat, deep fried, and covered with a warm sauce, often made with tomatoes.
chorizo	Spicy Mexican sausage served in various ways.
chuleta	Chop. Beef, pork, and lamb are common.

churros	Tubes of fried dough covered with sugar and usually eaten with hot chocolate.
cochinita pibil	Shredded pork served with a spicy sauce. It is a specialty of the Yucatán Peninsula.
dulce en almíbar	Preserved fruit served in a sugar syrup.
cnchiladas	A semi-fried corn *tortilla* most commonly filled with hot chicken and covered with cheese, some kind of sauce, and sometimes slices of raw onion.
flan	Rich custard topped with a caramel sauce; a favorite dessert throughout Mexico. The texture varies with the cook from breadlike to very delicate.
flautas	Crisp *tortillas* rolled into a tube shape, like a flute. They are stuffed with chicken, meat, cheese, or *refritos,* and served cold topped with cream, cheese, and lettuce.
flor de calabaza	Squash flowers, served in *quesadillas* or on their own.
frijoles	Beans. Some variety of this staple is served with most Mexican meals. The type or color of the beans served varies from region to region. Red, brown, black, and garbanzo beans (chick peas) are popular. *Frijoles* are often served boiled and spiced.
guacamole	A dip or spread made of mashed avocado with tomato, onion, *jalapeño* peppers, salt, and garlic. It is often served alongside spicy dishes to cool the tongue, but it is sometimes spicy as well.
huachinango al mojo de ajo	The fish red snapper fried or broiled with lots of chopped garlic, and generally served with the head and tail attached.
huitlacoche	Fungus taken from ears of corn. A real treat served in *quesadillas* or as a garnish or filling in a variety of dishes. Cream of *huitlacoche* soup is also popular.
machaca	Dried, shredded beef, sautéed and served with wheat flour *tortillas.* This dish is popular in the northern states, where it is sometimes served with eggs or in various sauces.
mariscos	Seafood, both fish and shellfish. Shrimp, oysters, squid, and octopus are all popular in coastal regions.
menudo	Pieces of intestines served in broth and accompanied by *tortillas.*

Milanesa	Breaded pork, beef, or chicken steak, fried and served with *tortillas.*
mole	A sauce made generally of nuts, *chiles,* and spices. It is usually poured over chicken, turkey, or *enchiladas.* There are various types. *Oaxaqueno* and *pipián moles* are popular. The most famous is *mole poblano* from Puebla, a truly Mexican dish blending chocolate with nuts, chiles, fruits, and spices.
nachos	*Tostadas* covered with melted cheese. In Mexico, *nachos* are sometimes prepared individually, topped with a piece of cheese and chiles which are then melted.
natilla	A thin custard pudding.
nopales	The new growth of a kind of cactus, most commonly served fresh in salads or grilled in *tacos.*
pan dulce	A sweet roll or Danish. There is a great variety of these in Mexico. They are typically bought fresh every day from the bakery.
pan	Bread. Aside from the traditional *tortilla,* there are all sorts of breads in Mexico, from delicious rolls to large loaves to sliced white and whole wheat bread in the style of the U.S. A visit to a bakery (*panería*), just as the bread is scheduled to come out of the oven, is a great experience, although you may encounter long lines. Mexicans prefer all their breads as fresh as possible.
pancita	Cow's stomach, served in a rich broth.
pozole	Hearty hominy soup made with shredded pork and garnished with lettuce, radishes, chopped onion and *chiles,* and oregano.
quesadillas	Fried *tortillas* filled with cheese. Many foods may be added, including *chiles,* chopped beef, potatoes, brains, squash flowers, *nopales,* and *huitlacoche.* They are usually served with spicy *salsa.*
queso fundido	Melted cheese, served with either corn or wheat *tortillas,* usually *tostadas.* It can be made with or without flavorings such as garlic, sausage, or chiles.
refritos	Refried beans, boiled, mashed, and then fried in oil or lard, sometimes with sausage.

romeritos	An herb, sort of resembling fresh-cut grass, prepared in a *mole* or other type of sauce.
salsa	Sauce. Unless it is served as part of a hot dish, *salsa* is generally a cold, spicy sauce made up of fresh chopped onion, tomato, herbs, and chili peppers. It may be red or green, depending on the *chiles* used, chunky or smooth, mild or fiery hot. Every restaurant and most cooks have their own special recipe. Bottled *salsas* similar to Louisiana Tabasco sauce are also common.
sopa	Soup. *Sopas* may be hot or cold, spicy or mild, clear, thin, chunky, or dry (*sopa seca,* which is not really dry but served as a hot dish like Spanish rice, rich with vegetables and sometimes meat). *Sopa de tortilla* is a common specialty.
sopes	A grilled *tortilla* covered with spicy *salsa,* cheese, and chopped onion.
tacos	Corn *tortillas* filled with meat to which *salsa* is often added. *Tacos* are the informal, traditional, and very common way to eat many meats. Depending on the region, they are typically made with soft or fried *tortillas.* In general, they are very different from the *tacos* popular in the U.S.
tamales	Corn meal wrapped and cooked in banana leaves or corn husks. Hot *tamales* are generally stuffed with a bit of chicken or pork and served warm; they are sometimes also spicy hot. Sweet *tamales* are served as a dessert flavored with sugar and often a bit of fruit.
tortas	A sandwich that looks a little like a turtle. Take one hard-crust roll, fill it with meat or cheese, tomato, avocado, onion, cream, and sliced chili pepper or *salsa.*
tortillas	A type of bread, basic to most Mexican meals. *Tortillas* are made of either ground corn or wheat flour (popular in the northern states of Mexico). Best served hot; when fried, they are called *tostadas.*
tostadas	Fried corn *tortillas,* typically served piled with shredded chicken or beef, tomatoes, lettuce, cream, chiles, cheese, and *salsa.*

*© 1986 by Kelly/Mooney.
Credit: Mexican
Government Tourism Office.*

Folkloric dancers in beautifully handmade, brightly colored costumes and traditional strolling bands with guitars, horns, and haunting voices, like these dancers and mariachis from Guadalajara, are enjoyed all over Mexico. The dances and styles change, but the rollicking, romantic spirit of Mexican folk music and dance has much in common from the cowboy north to the Mayan south. The art draws from both Spanish colonial and Native American traditions. Though there are wonderful regional variations and the music may be fast or slow, funny or full of romance, rustic, naughty, or edged with political rage, the theme is almost always the same: love and/or death embraced with a passion, a lust for life. Pop music from the North and from Europe is heard everywhere, but young Mexicans typically go for it, twist it, fill it with passion, and make it their own.

Some Books about Mexico

Brosnahan, Tom. *Frommer's Mexico on $20 a Day*. Simon & Schuster, New York, 1986.

Condon, John C. *Good Neighbors: Communicating with the Mexicans*. Intercultural Press, Yarmouth, Maine, 1985.

Fantini, Alvino E., and Beatriz C. de Fantini. *EIL Latin American Spanish* (with correlated tapes). The Experiment Press, Brattleboro, Vermont, 1967, revised 1986.

Fantini, Alvino E., and Beatriz C. de Fantini. *Living Language Travel-talk Spanish, Phrasebook and Dictionary*. Crown Publishers, Inc., New York, 1989.

Fantini, Alvino E., and Beatriz C. de Fantini. *Poly Training Tapes: Spanish*. Deutsche Grammophon Gesellschaft and The Experiment Press, Brattleboro, Vermont, 1972.

Franz, Carl. *People's Guide to Mexico*. John Muir Publications, Santa Fe, New Mexico, 1982.

Fodor's Mexico. David McKay Co., New York, annual.

Fuentes, Carlos. *The Death of Artemio Cruz*. Farrar, Straus & Giroux, New York, 1964.

Gordon, Raymond L. *Living in Latin America*. National Textbook Company, Chicago, Illinois, 1974.

Haas, Antonio, and Albano Guatti, photographer. *Mexico*. Scala Books, New York (distributed by Harper & Row), 1982.

Howells, John, and Don Merwin. *Choose Mexico: Live Well on $600 a Month*. Gateway Books: The Globe Pequot Press, 1997.

Heusinkveld, Paula. *Inside Mexico: Living, Traveling, and Doing Business in a Changing Society*. John Wiley & Sons, Inc. New York, 1994.

Kandell, Jonathan. *La Capital: The Biography of Mexico City*. Random House, New York, 1988.

Kras, Eva. *Management in Two Cultures: Bridging the Gap between U.S. and Mexican Managers*. Intercultural Press, Yarmouth, Maine, 1989.

Lewis, Oscar. *The Children of Sánchez*. Random House, New York, 1961.

Lewis, Oscar. *Five Families*. Mentor, New York, 1959.

Meyer, Michael C., and William L. Sherman. *The Course of Mexican History*, Fifth Edition. Oxford University Press, New York, 1995.

Oster, Patrick. *The Mexicans: A Personal Portrait of a People*. Harper & Row, New York, 1990.

Padgett, L. Vincent. *The Mexican Political System*. Houghton Mifflin, Boston, 1976.

Paz, Octavio. *The Labyrinth of Solitude: Life and Thought in Mexico*. Grove Press, New York, 1972.

Paz, Octavio. *El laberinto de la soledad*. Ediciones Cuadernos Americanos, Mexico, D.F., 1947.

Quirk, Robert. *Mexico*. Prentice Hall, Englewood Cliffs, New Jersey, 1971.

Riding, Alan. *Distant Neighbors: A Portrait of the Mexicans*. Vintage Books, New York, 1986.

Rodman, Seldon. *A Short History of Mexico*. Stein & Day, New York, 1982.

Simpson, Lesley Byrd. *Many Mexicos*. University of California Press, Berkeley, 1966.

For a travel packet with information and wholesale discounts for accommodations and travel, call the Mexican Tourist Bureau at 1-800-393-4634. Be prepared to say what part of Mexico you are interested in visiting and when.